Exploring Windows®8

FOR

DUMMIES®

by Galen Gruman, Mark Justice Hinton,
Woody Leonhard, and Andy Rathbone

Publisher's Acknowledgments

We're proud of this book; please send us your comments at http://dummies. custhelp.com. For other comments, please contact our Customer Care Department within the U.S. at 877-762-2974, outside the U.S. at 317-572-3993, or fax 317-572-4002.

Some of the people who helped bring this book to market include the following::

Acquisitions and Editorial

Senior Project Editor: Kim Darosett
Executive Editor: Steven Hayes
Copy Editor: Virginia Sanders
Editorial Manager: Leah Michael
Editorial Assistant: Leslie Saxman
Sr. Editorial Assistant: Cherie Case

Composition Services

Sr. Project Coordinator: Kristie Rees
Layout and Graphics: Ana Carrilo, Kathie Rickard, Rashell Smith, Erin Zeltner
Proofreader: Sossity R. Smith
Front Cover Photo: © Yaroslav Gavryliuk / iStockphoto
Back Cover Photo: © ViviSuArt / iStockphoto
Page 2: Image of PC: © Sandra Nicol / iStockphoto; image of tablet computer: © adam smigielski / iStockphoto; image of laptop: © 4X-image / iStockphoto

Publishing and Editorial for Technology Dummies

Richard Swadley, Vice President and Executive Group Publisher
Andy Cummings, Vice President and Publisher
Mary Bednarek, Executive Acquisitions Director
Mary C. Corder, Editorial Director

Publishing for Consumer Dummies

Kathleen Nebenhaus, Vice President and Executive Publisher

Composition Services

Debbie Stailey, Director of Composition Services

DUMMIES

Introduction

1 t's the biggest change to Windows since Windows XP debuted over a decade ago. It's also very much the same Windows you know from Windows 7. "It" is Windows 8, the new version of the most-used operating system on the planet.

What makes Windows 8 so radically different is its Start screen environment, which features big, bold tiles, full-screen applications, a simplified user interface, new ways of accessing features (such as through charms and the App bar), and support for touchscreen usage similar to the iPad.

What makes Windows 8 so familiar is that underneath that new Start screen environment lies the Windows Desktop, which is nearly identical to the Windows 7 you probably already use. It runs the apps you already know, and it works with files and the web the same way.

Using Windows 8 is very much like using two operating systems in one, and you switch between them based on the kind of apps you want to run: simple apps in the Start screen, complex ones in the Windows Desktop. This duality is particularly well suited for a tablet, where you can use the touch-oriented Start screen environment when on the road and then plug into a keyboard, mouse, and monitor when you're at a desk to get the full Windows 7 experience for apps such as Microsoft Office, Adobe Creative Suite, and QuickBooks.

Even better, it's not an either/or decision. You can use the full Windows Desktop on a touchscreen tablet — no mouse, keyboard, or monitor required. It just works better with them. Likewise, you can use the Start screen when connected to a mouse, keyboard, and monitor. It's just a little easier when you're using a touchscreen (which is why many new desktop PCs and laptops — not just tablets — will have touchscreens).

Windows 8 is Microsoft's way of embracing the new kind of computing that the iPhone and iPad introduced while remaining compatible with two decades' worth of Windows know-how and applications. Yes, it is a little confusing at first to have essentially two operating systems in one, but when you cross that bridge, you'll find richer land on the other side. This book helps you embrace the dual environments.

Getting Started with Windows 8

- *Exploring what's new in Windows 8*
- *Working with user accounts*
- *Setting up a password*

1 t's the Windows for everything: Windows 8 is the first version of Windows designed to run on desktop PCs, laptops, and touch-based PC tablets. To do that, it brings a whole new way of working with Windows called the Start screen environment (sometimes known by its code name, *Metro*). The Start screen is a sleek, tile-based user interface designed especially for touchscreen users and is based on Microsoft's Windows Phone operating system for smartphones. Keyboard-and-mouse users can work with the Start screen, too — it's the face of Windows that you see every time you start your PC.

But fear not: The familiar Windows 7 desktop remains available as well on almost all Windows PCs, and you'll use the Windows Desktop to run your familiar Windows applications, now called Windows Desktop apps. Essentially, you have two PCs in one with Windows 8 — the Start screen side and the Windows Desktop side — and you switch between the two as you use your PC, as explained later on.

What's New in Windows 8

Windows 8 is Microsoft's move to broaden Windows to tablets in a bid to compete with Apple's wildly popular iPad. And that means the adoption of the touch-oriented Start screen environment that debuted in 2010 in smartphones using Microsoft's Windows Phone operating system. Windows 8 is divided into these two environments:

- **Start screen:** This is now the environment you see first and that Microsoft hopes you'll use most. Its clean, simple tile interface and full-screen apps are easy to use after you get used to the new way of doing things. The People app gives you a unified place for all your social networking interactions. And Windows now displays notifications as they come in from your e-mail, messaging, and other apps, no matter what apps are in use.

- **Windows Desktop:** Although the Start screen and its apps represent the biggest changes to Windows, Microsoft has also enhanced the traditional desktop in Windows 8. After all, most people have a significant investment in Windows software that they don't want to throw away just because the Start screen environment is the new face of Windows. Plus, Start screen apps don't yet support the kind of complex operations that traditional Windows can — that's why Microsoft's new Office 2013 isn't a collection of Start screen apps but of traditional Windows apps.

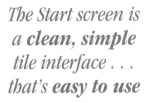

*The Start screen is a **clean, simple** tile interface . . . that's **easy to use***

Among the changes in the updated Windows Desktop:

- The Start button has been removed — you're supposed to use the Start screen as your starting point for accessing apps.

- Windows Explorer has been renamed File Explorer and now has a Ribbon that appears at the top of its window.

- Task Manager, where advanced users monitor what's happening in Windows, has gotten a lot more graphical.

And if you have multiple monitors connected to your PC, you can now share the same desktop background across them all. For touchscreen users, the new Start screen onscreen keyboard is much easier to use than the old Windows onscreen keyboard, and it's available in both the Start screen and the Windows Desktop environments.

Windows 8 boasts a new way to reinstall Windows that keeps your documents and data but resets Windows 8 to the factory defaults. You can still do a complete reinstall that wipes out everything if you prefer. The Windows Defender antivirus software is now included in Windows, and the File History feature backs up your data and settings automatically, so you can restore older copies of your files.

Most of the other changes are under the hood, including faster graphics performance, faster startup, and enhanced support for peripheral technologies such as USB 3.0 and cellular modems.

The Windows 8 Start screen (left) and the Windows 8 Desktop (right)

Working with User Accounts

When you start up Windows 8, you see a simple screen with a pretty picture and not much else. (The Start screen comes later.) It's called the *lock screen*. How do you unlock the lock screen? The answer depends on whether you're using a mouse, a keyboard, or a touchscreen:

- **Mouse:** On a desktop PC or laptop, click any mouse button.

- **Keyboard:** Press any key, and the lock screen slides away. Easy!

- **Touchscreen:** On a touchscreen display, touch the screen with your finger and then slide your finger up the glass. A quick flick of the finger will do.

The lock screen may show some status icons:

 Network connection enabled via Ethernet

 Wi-Fi connection enabled

 Battery status (for devices not connected via a power cord)

 Notifications from applications for new mail, calendar reminders, and the like

The lock screen is not simply a step in the way of getting into Windows. When coupled with a password, it ensures that no one else can use your computer or access its information. Even without a password, it works like a screensaver in that it hides what you're working on from any passersby. Windows 8 automatically locks the screen after a specified period of nonuse. You can manually lock the screen, as well: Click or tap your user icon in the Start screen and choose Lock from the pop-up menu, or press ⊞+L on a keyboard.

Signing in to your user account

After you've gotten past the lock screen, Windows wants you to *sign in* by clicking or tapping your name and typing in a password. Doing so signs you into your Windows user account, where all your files, programs, and settings reside.

You may have just one user account or several. For example, Windows lets you have a shared user account that synchronizes with all other PCs you have signed into via the same account, so every device is kept up-to-date. You can have a local account, which is not synchronized to other PCs you use. You can have both. (We explain how

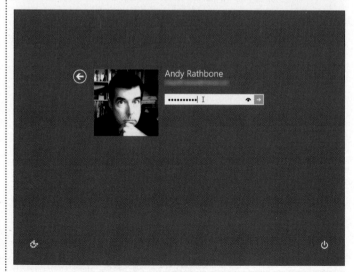

The Windows 8 lock screen (top), the Sign In screen for a PC with several user accounts, and the Sign In screen for a selected user

to create user accounts in the next section.) And multiple people can have accounts on the same PC, such as for a family or group of employees sharing a PC.

If you don't see a username listed for you on the Sign In screen, you have several options:

- **If you see your name and e-mail address listed, type your password.** Windows 8 lets you in and displays your Start screen, just as you last left it.

- **If you don't see your name, but you have an account on the computer, click or tap the left-pointing arrow shown in the margin.** Windows 8 displays a list of *all* the account holders. You may see the computer owner's name, as well as an Administrator account and a Guest account.

- **If you just bought the computer, use the account named Administrator.** Designed to give the owner full power over the computer, the Administrator account user can set up new accounts for other people, install programs, start an Internet connection, and access *all* the files on the computer — even those belonging to other people. Windows 8 needs at least one person to act as administrator.

- **Use the Guest account.** Designed for household visitors, this account lets guests, such as the babysitter or visiting relatives, use the computer temporarily.

- **No Guest account?** Then find out who owns the computer and beg that person to set up a username for you or to turn on the Guest account.

In addition to Administrator and standard accounts, Microsoft has another pair of account types, *Microsoft accounts* and *Local accounts.* So what's the difference? Each serves different needs:

- **Local account:** This account works fine for people working with traditional Windows programs on the Windows desktop. Local account holders can't run many of the Start screen apps bundled with Windows 8, including the Mail app. Nor can they download new apps from the Microsoft online store.

- **Microsoft account:** Consisting of an e-mail address and a password, this account lets you download apps from the Windows Store and run all the bundled apps in Windows 8. You can link a Microsoft account with your social media accounts, automatically stocking your address book with your friends from Facebook, Twitter, and other sites. (Plus, you can access both your own and your friends' Facebook photos.)

You can sign in with a Microsoft account in either of two ways:

- **Use an existing Microsoft account.** If you use Outlook.com, Hotmail, Windows Live, Xbox Live, or Windows Messenger, you already have a Microsoft account and password. Type in that e-mail address and password when setting up your user account and from then on in the Sign In screen.

- **Sign up for a new Microsoft account.** When creating or modifying a user account, click or tap Sign Up for a Microsoft Account, which opens a website where you can turn your existing e-mail address into a Microsoft account or, if you prefer, sign up for a new e-mail address for that account.

Until you customize your username picture, you'll see a silhouette. To add a photo to your user account, click or tap your username in the screen's corner and choose Change Account Picture. Click the Webcam button to take a quick shot with your computer's built-in webcam. No webcam? Then click Browse to peek through existing photos. *Hint:* Click or tap Files and choose Pictures to see all the photos on your PC.

If you have multiple user accounts, it's easy to switch among them: Click or tap your username or picture in the Start screen and choose Sign Out. The lock screen appears; click the screen or swipe up from the bottom edge to get the Sign In screen, click or tap the user account you want to sign in as, enter your password, and you're done!

Setting up and modifying user accounts

But how do you add and modify user accounts? Follow these steps:

1 Open the Charms bar and click or tap Settings.

The *Charms bar* is a small pane with a handful of icons, located on the right of the screen. Press ⊞+C (if you have a physical keyboard) to open the Charms bar. Or on a touchscreen, you can access it by swiping the right edge of the screen until the Charms bar appears: Put your finger off the screen on the right side and drag it toward the center.

2 Click or tap the Change PC Settings link.

3 Click or tap Users in the menu list at left and scroll down until the Add a User button is visible; click or tap it.

4 Enter an e-mail address to add a user who has a Microsoft account and click or tap Next. Or, to create a local account instead, click or tap Sign In without a Microsoft account, fill in the requested information on the screen that appears, and then click or tap Next.

5 If the account is for a child whose activity you want to monitor, select the Is This a Child's Account? option. Regardless, click or tap Finish to complete the setup.

DUMMIES

What else you can do on the Sign In screen

The Sign In screen offers two options unrelated to signing in to your account:

 The Accessibility icon (in the screen's bottom-left corner) customizes Windows 8 for people with physical challenges in hearing, sight, or manual dexterity. If you click or tap this button by mistake, click or tap on a different part of the screen to avoid changing any settings.

 The Power icon (in the screen's bottom-right corner) lets you shut down, put to sleep, or restart your PC. When you click or tap it, you get a menu with the Restart and Shut Down options; on a laptop or PC tablet, you may also see the Sleep option. (If you've accidentally shut down your PC, don't panic. Press your PC's power button, and your PC returns to this screen.) The Power button is also available via the Settings charm, described later on.

Setting a password for your user account

Because Windows 8 lets many people use the same computer, how do you stop Rob from reading Diane's love letters to Jason Bieber? How can Josh keep Grace from deleting his *Star Wars* movie trailers? Using a password solves some of those problems.

In fact, a password is more important than ever in Windows 8 because some accounts can be tied to a credit card. By typing a secret password when signing in, only you (or someone you entrusted with your password) can sign in to your account. If you protect your username with a password, nobody can access your files. And nobody can rack up charges for computer games while you're away from home.

When you create a user account, you're asked for a password. To change your password, click or tap the Settings charm, click Change PC Settings, click Users on the left side of the charm, and then click Change Your Password on the right side. Enter your new password (you need to enter it twice, to confirm you typed it correctly) and provide a hint that will be displayed should you enter an incorrect password several times. Click or tap Next and then click or tap Finish.

Rather than a password composed of letters and numerals, you can create a password that contains just numerals, known as a *PIN*, by selecting the Create a PIN option. A PIN is less secure than a password, and there is no reminder hint should you forget it.

Windows also offers the Create a Picture Password option in the Users pane of the Settings charm. Click or tap it and then, in the screen that appears, click Choose Picture to choose the image you want to appear. Then use your mouse or (on a touchscreen) your finger to draw the shape you want to use as your "password." You have to draw that same shape in the same location on the picture each time you need to sign in.

For your password, choose something like the name of your favorite vegetable, for example, or your dental floss brand. To beef up its security level, capitalize some letters and embed a number in the password, like **Glide2** or **Ask4More**. (Don't use either of those two examples, though, because they've probably been added to every password cracker's arsenal by now.) And remember that passwords are case-sensitive. The words *Caviar* and *caviar* are considered two different passwords.

If you don't want a password to sign in to your computer, you can disable the password feature — but that isn't recommended, because that means anyone can use your PC, its software, and its accounts. To disable passwords, click or tap the Change My Password option in the Users pane of the PC Settings screen, leave the New Password text field blank, and click or tap Next.

Using Windows 8 on Touchscreens

One of the big changes in Windows 8 is its extensive support for touchscreens. Previous versions of Windows have long supported pen-based (stylus) computing and even touchscreens, but, frankly, not well. In Windows 8, Microsoft has designed the Start screen environment explicitly for use on touchscreen devices and modified the Windows Desktop to be more touch-savvy.

Keyboard icon on the Windows Desktop taskbar

Use the Keyboard key to select different keyboards and to hide the keyboard

The Multiple Keyboards in Windows 8

The onscreen keyboard in Windows 8 is available in both the Start screen and Windows Desktop environments. In the Start screen, it appears automatically when you tap in a text field; in the Windows Desktop, it appears automatically only in Windows 8–savvy applications and must be manually opened from the taskbar in other applications, including Windows services such as the File Explorer and Control Panel.

The onscreen keyboard has several guises that you can switch among as needed, using its Keyboard key.

You can also set the onscreen keyboard to be fixed to the bottom of the screen or to be free-floating, so you can drag it around the screen. If the keyboard has space on either side, it is free-floating; if it extends to the both the left and right edges of the screen, it is fixed. The ability to move the onscreen keyboard is particularly useful on the Windows Desktop because dialog boxes and other controls don't move themselves from beneath the keyboard.

Close

Fix/Float Keyboard

The handwriting keyboard (for entering text via a pen)

Keyboard options

Hide Keyboard

Keyboard key

The standard, simplified onscreen keyboard

The split keyboard

The extended keyboard with all the keys of a physical keyboard

TIP

Press the &123 key to get a version of the standard keyboard with special symbols and numerals. Use the ← and → keys to switch between the two sets of available symbols. Press &123 again to get the standard alphabetic keyboard.

The Basic Gestures in Windows 8

Windows 8 has a small set of gestures you can use on a touchscreen to work with objects and the Windows 8 user interface. Note that a gesture functions only if an object is enabled to use that gesture; gestures are ignored otherwise.

Gesture	Name	Action
	Tap	Press a fingertip on the screen and then quickly pull it away from the screen. This action is used as a click or as the equivalent of pressing Enter.
	Drag	Press a fingertip on an object on the screen and then pull your finger across the screen to where you want to move the object to. If you drag a resizing handle or an object edge, you may resize the object instead.
	Swipe	Move one finger in a single direction, such as up or left. This action is used both for scrolling and to activate some Windows features, such as the Charms bar.
	Pinch	Hold your thumb and forefinger on the screen, apart from each other, and then draw them closer together. This action is used to zoom out (shrink the items).
	Expand	Hold your thumb and forefinger on the screen, close to each other, and then spread them apart. This action is used to zoom in (enlarge the items).
	Rotate	Place two fingertips on the screen near each other and then rotate your wrist to twist the fingers. This action rotates the selected item.

Setting Up a PC Tablet for Readability

Windows 8 is designed to run on a variety of devices, from PC tablets to desktop PCs with really big monitors. In the process, smaller devices got shortchanged — especially tablets. If you're much over 40, you'll probably find Windows 8 difficult to read on a PC tablet or other smaller screen (meaning anything smaller than 1,366 x 768 pixels) without reading glasses on. That's especially true of the Windows Desktop, which favors a cramped design that on a touchscreen device makes accurately tapping menu options and icons difficult, even when you can read them.

You can make Windows 8 friendlier to older eyes, however. You'll need to do so in two places: via the Settings charm in the Start screen half of Windows 8 and via the Control Panel on the Windows Desktop.

In the Settings charm, tap Change PC Settings, and in the Ease of Access pane, adjust the display by selecting the Make Everything on Your Screen Bigger option, if your tablet supports this option.

From the Windows Desktop, launch the Control Panel and go to the Display settings. In the Change the Size of All Items section, select Medium (125%) or, if available on your device, Larger (150%). You may want to further customize the text size in the Change Only the Text Size section by adjusting the individual UI elements via the pop-up menu below to at least 10 points.

Recommended settings for readability on a PC tablet for, the Start screen (left), and the Windows Desktop (right)

Working with the Start Screen

Every time you start up and sign in to your PC, switch user accounts, or sign in to your account after you or the PC has locked it, you get the Start screen.

The Start screen features live app tiles (top), the Recent Apps bar (bottom left) lets you switch among open applications, and the Charms bar (bottom right) provides quick access to common functions

The Start screen is where you access applications (such as the People app, the Mail app, and more) and change basic settings. From the Start screen, you can also switch to the Windows Desktop to configure more advanced settings (via the familiar Control Panel), access the Windows file system (via the File Explorer), and run traditional applications, such as Word or Excel. You can launch such applications from the Start screen, as described later. Doing so switches you automatically to the Windows Desktop.

Discovering the Start Screen

The Start screen works slightly differently depending on whether you're using a mouse or your finger to direct the action. (If needed, you can connect a mouse to a PC tablet via USB or Bluetooth.) Despite some differences in how you access them, the basic operations are the same:

✔ **Access the Charms bar.** Press ⊞+C (if you have a physical keyboard) to open the Charms bar. Or hover the mouse pointer over the bottom-right corner or top-right corner of the screen — called *hot corners* — until the charm icons appear, and then move the mouse into the Charms bar to have its background turn black and the charms' labels appear. On a touchscreen, swipe from the right edge of the screen to open the Charms bar. Charms provide quick access to common operations such as Search and Settings. Click or tap a charm to open it.

✔ **Access and switch among open apps.** Click or tap the Start charm to switch between the Start screen and open apps, including the Windows Desktop. Each click or tap cycles you to the next open item. You can also click the top-left or bottom-right hot corners of the screen. On a touchscreen, swipe from the screen's left edge to toggle the screen. You can also press the ⊞ key on a physical keyboard.

✔ **Open the Recent Apps bar.** If you hover the mouse pointer over either of the left hot corners or use your finger to swipe from the left edge and then drag back without releasing your finger from the screen, a thumbnail appears of the next recently opened item. Drag it out from the edge a little and then drag it back to the edge to open the Recent Apps bar that shows all recently open apps so you can select any one you want. You can also just press and hold ⊞+Tab and then click or tap the desired item.

✔ **Open the App bar.** Right-click the bottom of the screen or swipe up from the bottom of the screen to open the App bar. On the Start screen, there's just one icon on the App bar, All Apps, which shows tiles for all Windows applications and controls, not just the standard Start screen and Office apps and controls usually displayed on the Start screen.

✔ **Scroll the Start screen.** Scroll using the scroll bar or by swiping sideways anywhere on the screen to move among the tiles on the Start screen. Click or tap a tile to open its app. Use the Desktop tile to switch to the Windows Desktop.

✔ **Adjust sizing.** Click the Minimize icon to reduce the tiles' size to fit onscreen; on a touchscreen PC, use the pinch and expand gestures to zoom out and in, respectively.

✔ **Search for apps.** If you have a physical keyboard, you can start typing when the Start screen is visible to open the Search pane listing apps that match what you've typed so far. This is a handy way to find apps, both in the Start screen and in the Windows Desktop. Note that you can't use the onscreen keyboard for such searches on a tablet; use the All Apps option on the App bar or the Search charm instead.

The hot corners work only with a mouse, trackball, or other physical input device. They don't respond to taps on a touchscreen.

If you're running Windows 8 on a Mac via Boot Camp in OS X, Parallels Desktop, or EMC VMware's Fusion, you typically use the Mac ⌘ key or the Shift+⌘ combination as the equivalent of the PC ⊞ key.

You can disable the ability to switch among recent apps by going to the Settings charm's PC Settings, selecting the General pane, and setting the App Switching switch to Off.

Hot corner for the Start charm and Recent Apps bar

Charms bar

Hot corner to open the Charms bar

Hot corner for the Start charm and Recent Apps bar

Right-click for the App bar

Hot corner to open the Charms bar

Swipe down from top edge for the App bar

Swipe from left edge for the Start charm and Recent Apps bar

Charms bar (swipe from right edge)

Swipe up from bottom edge for the App bar

Swipe to left or right to navigate tiles (anywhere onscreen)

Pinch gesture to reduce file size or expand gesture to enlarge tile size (anywhere onscreen)

Using a mouse (top) or your finger (bottom) to work with the Start screen

In addition to the Charms bar and hot corners, the Start screen has *tiles.* A tile can be a live window into the application — commonly called an *app.* For example, a weather app's tile can show the current weather conditions, so you don't need to open the app to get the basic weather information. Likewise, a social network's tile can show current messages and posts. But a tile may be no more than an icon for its application; it need not have a live component.

Working with Tiles

The Start screen is — or should be — your one stop for the activities you do repeatedly. Because Windows 8 is split between two environments, the Start screen and Windows Desktop, you may believe that you can run only Start screen apps from the Start screen and only traditional Windows applications from the Windows Desktop. But that's not the case: You can launch both kinds of apps from the Start screen, as well as common Windows functions such as the Control Panel.

To close a Start screen app and return to the Start screen, press Alt+F4. Or just press ⊞ to switch back to the Start screen, leaving the app running in the background.

Adding and removing Start screen tiles

Tiles for Start screen apps that you buy are automatically added to the Start screen. So are Windows 8–savvy Windows Desktop apps such as Office 2013 and Google Chrome. But older Windows apps may need to be added manually. That means by you.

The App bar (at bottom) for the Start screen has one option: All Apps

To add apps or other functions to the Start screen, follow these steps for each item:

1 Open the Start screen's App bar by right-clicking a blank portion of the Start screen, or pressing ⊞+Z, or using a finger to swipe up from the bottom edge of the screen or swipe down from the top edge. Click or tap the All Apps icon.

2 Locate the app or control that you want to add a tile for on the Start screen.

3 Right-click the item you want to appear on the Start screen and click Pin to Start from the App bar that appears. On a touchscreen, drag the item to the bottom of the screen, release your finger from the screen, and tap Pin to Start from the App bar.

When you're finished adding apps, your Start screen will have grown considerably with all your newly added destinations.

To get rid of tiles on your Start screen, right-click an unwanted tile and click Unpin from Start from the App bar, or on a touchscreen, drag it to the bottom of the screen, release your finger from the screen, and tap Unpin from Start.

TIP

From the App bar, you also can pin apps and functions to the Windows Desktop taskbar for easy access. To do so, use the same steps you used for adding them to the Start screen, but click or tap Pin to Taskbar instead. This option appears only for apps and services that can run on the Windows Desktop. Note that you can't pin Windows Desktop apps to the Start screen from the Windows Desktop.

Arranging and grouping Start screen tiles

Everyone seems to have a personal style of organizing their computer's desktop and files (including *not* organizing them!). So, as you'd expect, the Start screen lets you organize its tiles. But if you've used previous versions of Windows, OS X, Android, or iOS, you'll find that the Start screen offers some differences that set it apart from those operating systems' old-school approaches.

Like other operating systems, the Windows 8 Start screen lets you rearrange tiles by dragging them to different locations on the screen. When you drop a tile on or between others, they make room for the new tile.

But what's different about the Start screen is that some tiles — those with live previews — can be of two different sizes: a wide rectangle and a smaller square. Other tiles are always squares.

rearrange tiles by dragging them . . . on the screen

To change the size of a tile:

- On a PC, right-click the tile and click the Smaller or Larger icon on the App bar. (Wide tiles have the Smaller option, whereas square tiles have the Larger option.)

- On a touchscreen, drag the tile to the bottom of the screen, release your finger to open the App bar, and then tap the Smaller or Larger icon.

The Start screen's tiles can become hard to navigate as you add apps because the set of tiles to scroll through gets longer and longer. It sure would be nice to be able to group them . . . and you can! (However, you can't create folders of application tiles, as you can in other operating systems and on the Windows Desktop.)

When first installed, the Windows 8 Start screen includes two unlabeled groups of tiles, with a narrow space between the two groups. That small space is how you know where one group ends and the next begins.

The App bar (at bottom) lets you narrow or widen live tiles. In the tiles area, note the wider gap between tiles that separates tile groups.

Follow these steps to create and name a group of tiles:

1 To create a new group, drag and drop a tile into the gap between two existing groups. A vertical bar appears, letting you know a new group will be created in that space.

2 To add more tiles to your newly created group, drag and drop additional tiles into the group. You can drag the tiles within the group to arrange them as desired.

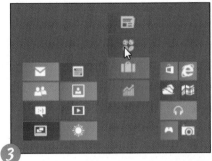

3 Rearrange the groups as desired. If you're using a mouse, click the – icon in the Start screen's bottom-right corner to switch to a reduced-size group view of the tiles, or if you're using a touchscreen, use the pinch gesture to get that view. Drag from anywhere in a group to move in the entire group.

4 (Optional) To name a group, in the group view right-click the group you want to name and click the Name Group icon on the App bar. On a touchscreen, drag the group to the bottom of the screen and then tap Name Group. When the Name text field appears, type a name and then click or tap the Name button.

5 Return from the group view to the standard Start screen by clicking in the screen or using the expand gesture.

Customizing the Start Screen

In addition to arranging your tiles, Windows 8 lets you adjust other aspects of the Start screen, such as the background, color scheme, and text size. You do so via the Settings charm.

After clicking or tapping the Settings charm, click the words Change PC Settings. In the window that appears, a list of panes appears at left; the settings for each pane appear at right, and you'll likely have to scroll to see them all.

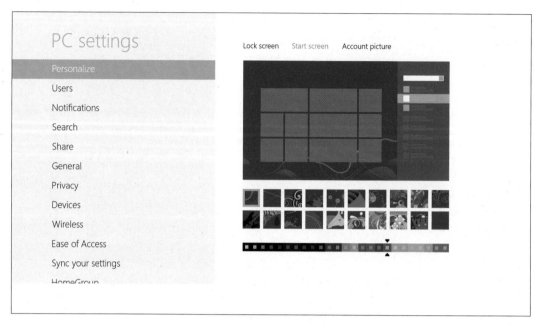

The Start Screen options in the Personalize pane of the PC Settings window

The Personalize pane is where you set the color scheme and background for the Start screen, change the background image for the lock screen, and select what image to use with your user account.

The Personalize pane is pretty simple to use: Click the squares for the color scheme and background pattern you want. That's it — as in all Start screen settings, there's no OK or Apply or Done button to click or tap, because all changes are applied immediately.

The Lock Screen pane is a little more complex, but not much. Click or tap an image to use as the lock screen background or click Browse to choose your own. But there's more! You may need to scroll down a bit to see the Lock Screen Apps section, where you specify which apps show notifications in the lock screen. By default, Mail, Calendar, and Messaging are already configured to do so. Click a + icon to add an app whose notifications you want to see in the lock screen; you can have as many as six. To remove an app from the lock screen notifications, click its icon and then choose Don's Show Quick Status Here from the menu that appears.

The Lock Screen options in the Personalize pane of the PC Settings window

✔ **The Notifications pane** lets you specify which applications can display notifications in the upper right of the Start screen and the Windows Desktop. Here, you use the On/Off switches to set whether notifications appear in Windows 8 and/or on the lock screen, as well as whether a tone plays with them. Below those three options, you select which applications are allowed to notify you.

✔ **The Ease of Access pane** lets you make changes to appearance. It's aimed at users with disabilities, but one option may tempt many users: Make Everything on Your Screen Bigger. The Start screen environment has big tiles, but

often text is hard to read for older eyes. This setting makes everything bigger, as it promises, but in doing so it can change how settings and other charms display: Instead of showing a list of panes at left and the options at right, the magnified charms may show one or the other, depending on your screen resolution. If you see just the list of panes, click or tap one to see its settings, but the list is gone. To get back, click or tap the icon of a left arrow in a circle at the upper left of the screen. Unfortunately, the Make Everything on Your Screen Bigger option is disabled on many tablets, which could really use this option given their relatively small screens.

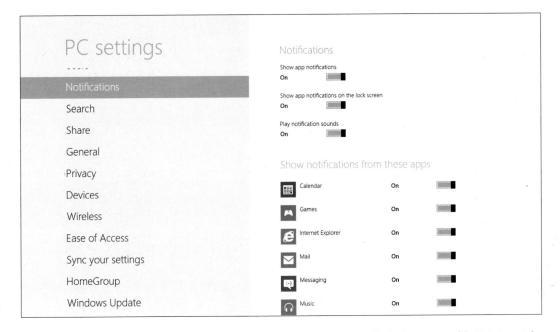

The Notifications pane of the PC Settings window

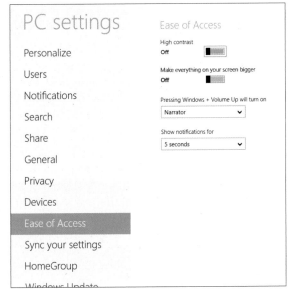
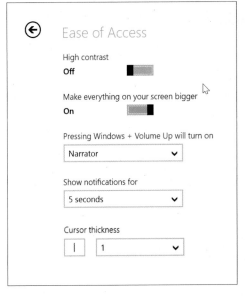

With Make Everything on Your Screen Bigger enabled, Windows 8 may have to separate the list of panes from a pane's options on a smaller display, as shown at right

Working with Charms

Charms are a Windows 8 feature designed to give you quick access to commonly used functions. You can open the Charms bar in a few different ways. Press ⊞+C if you're using a physical keyboard. If you're using a mouse, hover the mouse pointer over either of the right hot corners until the charm icons appear and then move the mouse into the Charms bar to have its background turn black and the charms' labels to appear. On a touchscreen, swipe from the right edge of the screen to open the Charms bar.

The Search charm (at left) and the Settings charm (at right)

Windows 8 makes five charms available on the Charms bar:

 Search: Click or tap this charm to search through whatever application is active onscreen. To expand your search, choose one of the other search locations: Apps, Settings, or Files. Or choose another of the apps listed. *Shortcut:* Press ⊞+Q or, to do a file search, ⊞+F.

 Share: Click or tap this charm to share what's currently in your application, assuming it is a sharable item. When viewing a web page, for example, the Share charm lets you choose Mail to e-mail the page's link to a friend. Use the Share pane in the Settings charm's PC Settings to specify which apps appear here. *Shortcut:* Press ⊞+H.

 Start: Click or tap this charm to cycle through open applications and the Start screen, as described earlier. Shortcut: Press ⊞+Tab.

 Devices: Click or tap this charm to send your current screen's information to another device, such as a printer, second monitor, or perhaps a phone. The Devices option lists only devices that are currently connected with your computer and able to receive the screen's information. *Shortcut:* Press ⊞+K.

 Settings: Click or tap this charm to tweak your computer's six major settings by clicking or tapping the desired setting's icon: Wi-Fi/Network, Volume, Screen, Notifications, Power, and Keyboard/Language. Click or tap Change PC Settings to adjust other settings, such as notifications, background, privacy, user accounts, and Windows update. *Shortcut:* Press ⊞+I.

The following three charms vary their options based on what app is currently open onscreen:

- **Search:** When a Start screen app is onscreen, by default it searches that app. Whether the Start screen or the Windows Desktop is active, by default it searches for apps. In all cases, you can always choose to search the PC, the web, or a specific app instead from the charm.

- **Share:** When a Start screen app is onscreen and sharable content is selected or active, it lets you share that content via compatible services such as e-mail and social networking. When no compatible content is active, the charm notes that nothing is available to be shared. Likewise, whether the Start screen or the Windows Desktop is active, it notes that nothing is sharable.

- **Settings:** When a Start screen app or the Start screen is active, the top of the charm shows links specific to that app or the Start screen; tap a link to open a pane showing available settings. For the Windows Desktop, the charm shows three links that open various parts of the Control Panel: Control Panel (the top level showing all control panels), Personalization, and PC Info.

Time-saving shortcuts in Windows 8

Action	Shortcut	Gesture
Go to Start screen	⊞	Swipe from right edge, tap Start
Switch among active apps	⊞+Tab	Swipe from left edge
Switch to Windows Desktop	⊞+D	None
Open the App and Control bars	⊞+Z	Swipe from top or bottom edge
Open Charms bar	⊞+C	Swipe from right edge
Open Search charm	⊞+Q	Swipe from right edge, tap Search
Open Search charm to Files	⊞+F	None
Open Search charm to Settings	⊞+W	None
Open Share charm	⊞+H	Swipe from right edge, tap Share
Open PC Settings	⊞+I	None
Open Windows Desktop	⊞+D	None
Switch to Windows Desktop	⊞+B	None
Open File Explorer	⊞+E	None
Open Power User menu	⊞+X	None
Reduce Start screen app to right side	⊞+. (period)	None
Reduce Start screen app to left side	⊞+Shift+. (period)	None
Move Start screen to next display*	⊞+PgDn	None
Move Start screen to previous display*	⊞+PgUp	None
Copy	Ctrl+C	Tap and hold on image or text selection handle, choose Copy
Paste	Ctrl+V	Tap and hold in destination, choose Paste
Cut	Ctrl+X	None
Zoom in	None	Expand thumb and forefinger
Zoom out	None	Pinch thumb and forefinger
Lock the screen	⊞+L	None

* For PCs with multiple monitors in use

Working with the Windows Desktop

- What's different on the Windows Desktop
- Touring the taskbar and application window
- Opening the Windows Desktop
- Sizing and moving windows

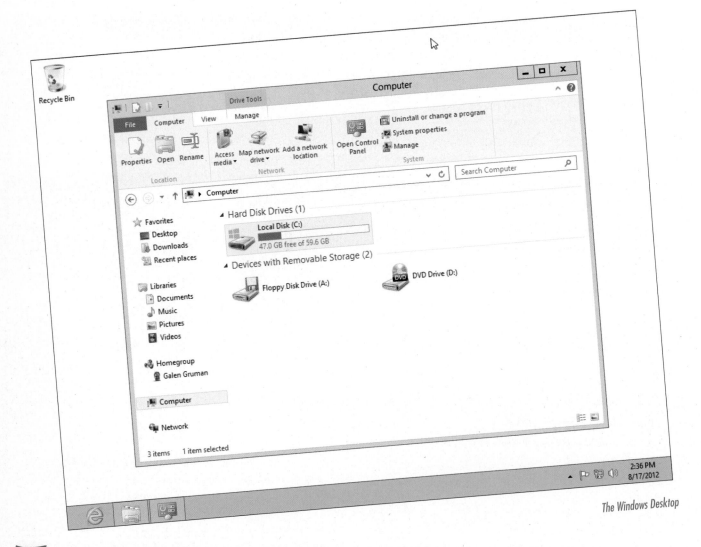

The Windows Desktop

The Start screen is new to Windows, so it's a little mysterious. But if you've used previous versions of Windows — and most people have — the Windows Desktop part of Windows 8 will be very familiar. It's basically Windows 7 with a few changes:

✔ **There is no Start menu.** The only way to quickly access items when in the Windows Desktop is to pin them to the taskbar at the bottom of the screen after you've opened them. (Right-click or tap and hold an open application's icon to get a menu that lets you pin it to the taskbar.)

DUMMIES

✏ **The File Explorer, the file manager called Windows Explorer in Windows 7, is always pinned to the taskbar.** You can navigate your PC's files the normal way, through the file hierarchy and search capabilities. Also use File Explorer to find your applications not pinned to the taskbar.

✏ **Internet Explorer 10 is also always pinned to the taskbar.** Note that the IE 10 version in the Windows Desktop is not the same as the IE 10 in the Start screen; the Windows Desktop one has more capabilities, such as full support for Oracle Java and Adobe Flash.

✏ **When using a PC tablet, you usually must activate the onscreen keyboard whenever you want to use it.** The keyboard doesn't usually automatically appear when you tap a text field, as it always does in the Start screen portion of Windows 8. Windows 8–savvy applications such as Office 2013 and Google Chrome do open the keyboard for you in the Windows Desktop when you tap a text field. Tap the Keyboard button on the taskbar to open the onscreen keyboard yourself, and tap its Close box to hide it.

✏ **The left hot corners used with a mouse work differently in the Windows Desktop than in the Start screen.** The bottom-left hot corner only switches you to the Start screen; you can't use it to switch among recent apps or open the Recent Apps bar — only the top-left hot corner can do that in the Windows Desktop.

✏ **In the C: drive, you may notice two Windows folders — Program Files and Program Files (x86) — instead of the Program Files folder in previous versions of Windows.** The Program Files folder contains Windows 8 native applications, whereas the Program Files (x86) folder contains apps designed only for Windows 7 and earlier.

Here's how to use the hot corners in the Windows Desktop:

① Switch to the Start screen by hovering your pointer over the lower-left corner and then clicking the thumbnail that appears.

② Switch to the next recently open app by hovering your pointer over the upper-right corner and then clicking the thumbnail that appears.

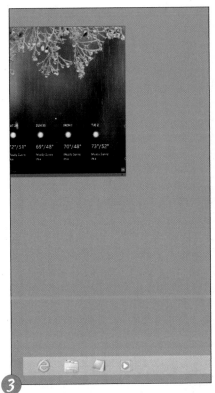

③ (Optional) Pull out the thumbnail that appears until it replaces the Windows Desktop with the thumbnail's app and then release the mouse button.

Getting to the Windows Desktop

So how do you get to the Windows Desktop from the Start screen? There are several methods:

- Use the keyboard shortcut ⊞+D to launch the Windows Desktop or ⊞+E to launch the Windows Desktop with the File Explorer file manager active.

- Click or tap the Desktop tile.

- If you previously opened the Windows Desktop and then moved to the Start screen or a Start screen app, you can switch back to the Desktop through one of these methods:

  - Use the Start charm or press ⊞+Tab to cycle among the Start screen and open apps, including the Desktop (if it's open).

- With a mouse, hover over one of the left hot corners, pull out the thumbnail that appears, and drag it back to the left side to display the Recent Apps bar; then click the Windows Desktop's thumbnail. On a touchscreen, you get the thumbnail by sliding in from the left edge of the screen.

A tablet running Windows RT has only a limited version of the Windows Desktop. It can run only the Start screen part of Windows 8 and Start screen applications, as well as a special version of Office 2013 and IE 10 that Microsoft pre-installs in Windows RT tablets. You can also use File Explorer to navigate files.

Touring the Taskbar

The taskbar is the command center for the Windows Desktop. It's where you can most easily work with applications, and it gives you quick access to various services such as network settings, date and time, Windows Update, and other Windows capabilities.

Any running Windows Desktop apps (such as Word or Windows Media Player) display their icon on the taskbar. Click or tap the icon to switch to that app; if the app is open, clicking or tapping it minimizes the app (leaves it running but hides it). Likewise, click or tap an icon in the right end of the taskbar to open its service, such as changing network settings, adjusting speaker volume, or opening the Action Center to check for system updates.

Here's what else the taskbar can do:

- **Live application preview:** Hover the mouse pointer or quickly tap the icon to see a preview of the app's current status, if it's running.

- **Pinned to Taskbar:** You can keep app icons permanently available for future use by pinning them to the taskbar. To pin an app to the taskbar, right-click the icon on the taskbar (on a touchscreen, tap and hold the icon) and from the menu that appears choose Pin to Taskbar. (Choose Unpin from Taskbar to remove it.)

A live application preview

- **An application's contextual menu:** Right-click or tap and hold an app icon to get a contextual menu with available options — called a *jump list* — for that app, such as to switch to a specific application window, run a task, or close (quit) the app. (This is the same menu where you pin or unpin an app.) Note that not all apps have jump list options.

On a touchscreen, it can be hard to open an application's contextual menu by tapping and holding or to see its preview by tapping it. You're better off using a physical mouse for such actions.

An application's contextual menu

✔ **Icon Tray Settings menu:** Click or tap the up-pointing triangle icon on the taskbar to get a list of hidden icons and to get the Customize option that lets you change what displays in the icon tray.

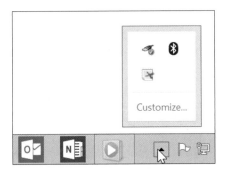

The Icon Tray Settings menu

✔ **Desktop Settings menu:** Right-click or tap and hold on the desktop right above the taskbar to open the Desktop Settings menu of common display settings, such as changing the screen resolution, adjusting how icons display and file names are sorted, and opening the Personalize control panel to change the desktop's look.

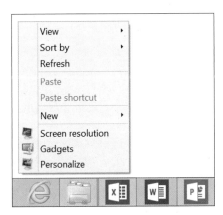

The Desktop Settings menu

✔ **Toolbar Settings menu:** Right-click or tap and hold on an empty areas in the taskbar to open the Toolbar Settings menu that lets you add

toolbar items to the taskbar such as for opening recently open web links, the onscreen keyboard, and the desktop (which hides all open apps). You also can set how windows display on the desktop: side by side (stacked) or overlapping (cascading).

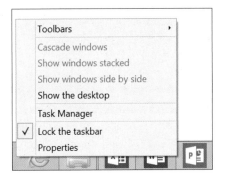

The Power User menu

✔ **Power User menu:** Hover the mouse pointer over the lower-left corner until the Start screen thumbnail appears and then right-click it to open the new Power User menu, which lets you quickly open pro-level features such as the command prompt, administrator tools, and the Device Manager.

The Toolbar Settings menu

TIP

You can customize the look and feel of the Windows Desktop. For example, to change the background, choose Personalize from the Desktop Settings menu to open the Personalization control panel. From there, you can choose an existing theme from those displayed, or you can scroll down to find more options.

Touring the Application Window

When you run an application or Windows service in the Windows Desktop environment, you'll see it in an application window, which provides both standard controls and additional controls for each application.

TIP

Scan the edges of application windows because important information and functions are often pushed to these edges around the main content area.

Here's a quick review of the standard controls:

✔ **Quick Access toolbar:** This gives you fast access to common operations, such as saving a document. This toolbar is not present in all windows and may feature different functions, depending on the window.

✔ **Title bar:** The top line of the window contains the title of the desktop program you're using. When you use a program to create a document, the name of the document also appears in the title bar.

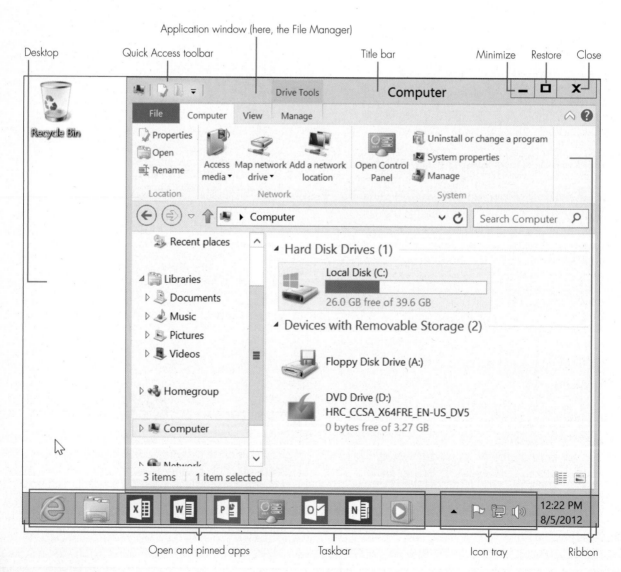

Application window (here, the File Manager)

Desktop   Quick Access toolbar   Title bar   Minimize   Restore   Close

Drive Tools   Computer

File   Computer   View   Manage

Properties   Access media ▾   Map network drive ▾   Add a network location   Open Control Panel   Uninstall or change a program
Open   System properties
Rename   Manage

Location   Network   System

◀ ▶ Computer   Search Computer

Recent places

▲ Libraries
  ▷ Documents
  ▷ Music
  ▷ Pictures
  ▷ Videos

▷ Homegroup

▷ Computer

▷ Network

▲ Hard Disk Drives (1)

Local Disk (C:)
26.0 GB free of 39.6 GB

▲ Devices with Removable Storage (2)

Floppy Disk Drive (A:)

DVD Drive (D:)
HRC_CCSA_X64FRE_EN-US_DV5
0 bytes free of 3.27 GB

3 items   1 item selected

12:22 PM
8/5/2012

Open and pinned apps   Taskbar   Icon tray   Ribbon

Recycle Bin

FOR DUMMIES

✔ **Minimize:** This shrinks or hides the window's contents. The program that the window contains is still running and open, but the window is out of sight. You'll still see the program's icon in the taskbar. To restore the window, click or tap its icon on the taskbar.

✔ **Maximize/Restore:** If the button's icon is a single square, it's the Maximize button, and clicking or tapping it fills the screen with the contents of the window. If the icon shows two squares, it's the Restore button, and clicking or tapping it returns the window to its previous size

✔ **Close:** Click or tap this button to close (quit) the application. You can also press Alt+F4.

✔ **Ribbon:** Below the title bar, starting at the left edge of the window, is the Ribbon, a toolbar organized as tabbed panes that provides access to many functions via menus and icons. The tabs appear across the top of the Ribbon; click the tab label to switch to it. Although Ribbons vary among programs, most Ribbons have File, Home, and View tabs. (In Windows 8, File Explorer now has a Ribbon, but it's hidden by default: Click or tap a tab label to open it.)

✔ **Status bar:** Along the bottom edge of the window, some programs display information about the window or its contents in a single-line *status bar*. (File Explorer does not have a status bar.)

TIP

You can press ⊞+↑ to maximize the current window. And you can press ⊞+↓ to restore a maximized window or to minimize a window that is not maximized.

TIP

Display or hide the Ribbon's tabs by pressing Ctrl+F1 or clicking or tapping the ^ icon on the far right, next to the Help icon (the question mark). Each time you do so, the Ribbon's tabs switch between being displayed and hidden. The tab labels always remain visible.

Resizing and Arranging Windows

You can move a window on the desktop by dragging the title bar with a mouse or, on a touchscreen, with your finger. Likewise, you can resize a window by dragging any of its sides or corners to both resize and reshape it in the direction you drag the side or corner.

But Windows also offers other methods. One is called *snapping a window*. Drag a window to the left or right edge of the screen. When the mouse or your finger touches the edge of the screen, you'll see an outline on the screen. Release the window, and it resizes automatically to fill that half of the screen. You can also press ⊞+→ to snap to the left side or press ⊞+← to snap to the right side.

Here are a few more sizing tricks you can try:

✔ Drag a snapped window by the title bar away from the edge of the screen to return the window to its previous size.

✔ Drag a window (snapped or not) to the top edge of the screen to maximize the window.

✔ Drag the title bar of a maximized window away from the top to restore it to its previous size.

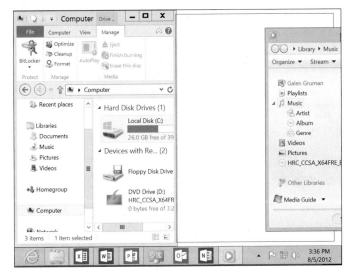

A snapped window on the left and a window being snapped on the right

Using Start Screen Apps

● *Opening and closing Start screen apps* ● *Accessing options and settings in apps*
● *The Start screen's included apps*

*J*ust as Windows 8 has the Start screen and Windows Desktop environments, so too does it have apps that run in these respective environments. Windows 8 comes with a bunch of Start screen apps, and you can add more from the Windows Store, an app that is the only place you can buy and download Start screen apps from.

The Start screen shows tiles for each Start screen app that is installed. It may also have tiles for Windows Desktop apps that come installed on a new computer. You can see even more tiles if you open the App bar in the Start screen (right-click the bottom of the screen or swipe up from the bottom of the screen) and click or tap the All Apps icon. This All Apps view of the Start screen shows tiles for a variety of Windows Desktop apps and services such as Calculator, the Control Panel, Notepad, and Remote Desktop Connection.

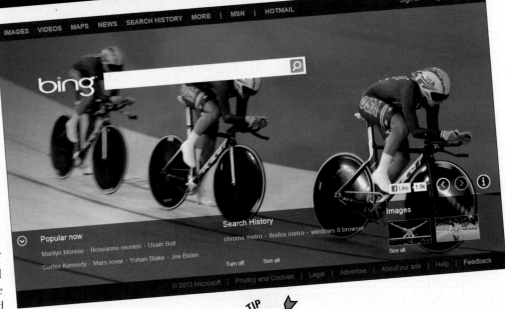

TIP

To see the administrator tools — specialty apps that power users often use — from the Windows Desktop in the Start screen, open the Settings charm, click or tap Tiles at the top of the Charms bar, and then set the Show Administrative Tools switch to Yes. Click outside the Settings charm to close it.

Opening and Closing Apps

Here's how to open an app from its Start screen's tile:

- ✔ **Mouse:** Click the tile.

- ✔ **Keyboard:** Press the arrow keys until a box surrounds the desired tile. Then press the Enter key.

- ✔ **Touchscreen:** Tap the tile.

To close an app you're currently working in, point the mouse at the screen's top edge. When the mouse pointer turns into a hand, hold down the mouse button and drag the app toward the screen's bottom. When the mouse reaches the screen's bottom edge, you've closed the app; release your finger from the screen. You can also press Alt+F4 if you have a keyboard.

On a touchscreen, drag your finger from the top edge of the screen all the way to the bottom edge; the app's screen should shrink about halfway through. When you reach the bottom, the app is tossed away and closed. (The Alt+F4 shortcut and the throwaway gesture tricks work on the Windows Desktop, as well.)

Working with App Options

In the Start screen environment, all apps run in full-screen mode, so there's nothing to distract you. But when you need to work on the application's settings or additional options, you can summon them. To do so, right-click in any empty portion of the app (outside any controls or fields) or swipe up from the bottom edge of the screen or down from the top edge of the screen.

The App and Control bars

Almost all Start screen apps have the App bar at the bottom of the screen (the Store app is an exception). The App bar displays one or more icons that you can click or tap to open a menu, a dialog box, or another interface element that exposes their capabilities.

In addition, some apps also have the Control bar at the top of the screen, which offers even more capabilities, usually to help you navigate. It displays when you open the App bar. For example, the Start screen version of Internet Explorer 10 uses the Control bar to show recently open web pages so

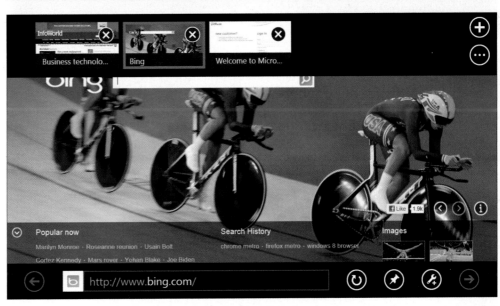

The Weather app (top) and Internet Explorer 10 app (bottom) with their App and Control bars visible

you can quickly reopen them. And the Weather app uses the Control bar to provide navigation to different features within the app.

The Settings charm

There's one more place you may find app options: the Settings charm. When you open the Settings charm while an app is onscreen, the Settings charm shows any links to options for that app at top. Click or tap a link to open its corresponding settings pane. For example, the Weather app's Preferences pane lets you choose between Celsius and Fahrenheit and specify whether your search history for locations is saved (for easy access later to those locations). And IE 10's Internet Explorer Settings pane lets you delete the browser history, control whether your location is shared with websites, set the zoom level, and enable rightward scrolling to flip to the next page in a multipage web page.

All apps' Settings charms have a Permissions link that shows the resources (such as location and access to your contacts) that the app uses, along with switches that let you disable such permissions for that app. Note that disabling permissions can interfere with the app's ability to function properly, but some apps may be accessing personal information they don't really need, such as to send ads to your friends or track your location to build a profile of your activities, so it's always a good idea to check the permissions for each new app you install.

Navigating within Apps

When you use the scroll bar to move to the right or, on a touchscreen, when you swipe to the right, many apps reveal more information about their current content. (Depending on the screen resolution and display settings, you may see part of the adjacent information onscreen to help you realize it exists.) Swipe to the left to scroll back.

For example, scrolling sideways in Internet Explorer 10 moves you among open browser windows, and doing so in the Weather app shows you more details for the current location, such as historical weather data and screens that show global weather. Scroll or swipe sideways to move back and forth through this additional information. Whether and how apps use this additional screen real estate varies from app to app.

Many applications display tiles or menus to open additional content. For example, the People app's What's New pane shows tiles for recently received tweets and Facebook posts. Click or tap a content tile or a menu item to open the content. To get back to that menu or tile list, click or tap the left-arrow icon in the upper left of the screen; it's essentially a Back button.

Three charms usually provide custom options when you're in an app. The *Search* charm lets you search within the app's contents, as well as search the web, your PC, or other apps' contents. The *Share* charm lets you share the app's current information via e-mail or social networking, such as for text, URLs, and images (in apps that support sharing). The *Settings* charm lets you set preferences and other behaviors for the current app.

Scrolling through an app's extended screen

Running Multiple Apps

The Start screen is designed to run one app at a time. Well, not quite: Multiple apps can be running, but you work with only one at a time due to the full-screen nature of Start screen apps. Well, again not quite. Windows 8 provides a way to display two apps on screen at the same time. You need a physical keyboard to make this work, but it's quite easy to do: Press ⊞+. (period) to reduce the current app to a strip on the right side of the screen. (Or you can press ⊞+Shift+. [period] instead to reduce it to the left side.) Then go to the Start screen to open a desired app (including the Windows Desktop) to have it appear onscreen next to the other app's strip.

You can use both apps when they're side by side, and if you want to make the smaller window larger, drag the dividing line between the two apps or press ▦+. (period) or ▦+Shift+. (period) again to change the view: It first reverses the two windows' sizes and, if pressed again, makes the larger window full-screen again.

Running two apps side by side

Finding the Apps You Want to Use

Your Start screen will change as you add more programs and apps to your computer. That's why the Start screen on your friend's computer, as well as in the figures shown here, is probably arranged differently than your computer's Start screen.

You can scroll through the Start screen until your eagle eyes spot the tile you need, and then you can pounce on it with a quick click or tap. But when the thrill of the hunt wanes, Windows 8 offers several shortcuts for finding apps and programs hidden inside a tile-stuffed Start screen:

- **Mouse:** Mouse users can right-click on a blank portion of the Start screen. The App bar appears on the screen showing an icon named All Apps. Click the All Apps icon to see an alphabetical listing of *all* your computer's apps and programs. Click the desired app or program to open it.

- **Touchscreen:** On a touchscreen, slide your finger up from the screen's bottom edge. When the App bar appears, tap the All Apps icon to see an alphabetical list of all your apps and programs.

- **Keyboard:** While looking at the Start screen, users of physical keyboards can simply begin typing the name of the desired app or program, like this: **facebook**. As you type, Windows 8 lists all the apps matching what you've typed so far, eventually narrowing down the search to the runaway.

No matter what input devices you use, you also can open the Search charm, click or tap the Apps icon, and enter the desired app's name in the Search box; then press Enter or click or tap the Search button (magnifying-glass icon). Click or tap the app's icon from the results pane to open it.

As you open applications, how do you switch among them from the Start screen? After all, there is no taskbar of open applications as in the Windows Desktop. There are several ways, which work both on the Start screen and on the Windows Desktop:

- **Press ▦+Tab** on your keyboard to switch to the next open application; keep pressing the key to cycle through the open apps.

- **Press ▦ or click or tap the Start charm** to switch between the Start screen and the last-used app.

- **Open the Recent Apps bar to see a list of icons for all open apps**. The Recent Apps bar is, essentially, a taskbar that works in both the Start screen and Windows Desktop environments showing all open apps, whether the Start screen or Windows Desktop. (The Windows Desktop's taskbar shows only non–Start screen apps.)

To open this bar, just press ▦+Tab, hold ▦, and then click or tap the desired app from the bar that appears on the left side of the screen. You can also hover the mouse pointer over the upper-left hot corner, or you can swipe from the left edge and then drag back without releasing your finger from the screen. A thumbnail appears of the next open item. Pull it out from the edge a little and then drag it back to the edge to open the Recent Apps bar.

The Apps That Come with the Start Screen

The following Start screen apps are preinstalled with Windows 8, whether you get a new PC or upgrade from a previous version of Windows:

- **Bing:** This app lets you do a basic web search. Frankly, you get more search controls if you go to **www.bing.com** or **www.google.com** in Internet Explorer.

- **Calendar:** This lets you add your appointments or grab them automatically from calendars already created through accounts with Google or Hotmail.

- **Camera:** This lets you snap photos with your computer's built-in camera or an attached camera.

- **Desktop:** Choose this to fetch the traditional Windows Desktop.

- **Finance:** This live tile shows a 30-minute delay of the current Dow, NASDAQ, and S&P stock indices. The app itself shows more-detailed charts and current financial news, tracks specific stocks you enter, and lets you convert currencies and check interest rates.

- **Games:** Designed for Xbox 360 owners, this app lets you see your achievements, friends, and played games. Plus, you can watch game trailers and buy new games for your console.

- **Internet Explorer:** The Start screen mini-version of Internet Explorer browses the web full-screen. Note that it does not support plug-ins such as Adobe AIR; use the full version of IE 10 in the Windows Desktop for such complete browsing capabilities. (Adobe Flash is supported, but there's no plug-in that you need to install: Microsoft has folded Adobe's Flash into IE 10 itself.)

- **Mail:** This app lets you send and receive e-mail. If you enter a Hotmail/Outlook.com or Google account, the Mail app sets itself up automatically, stocking your People app's address list from your contacts as well.

- **Maps:** Handy for trip planning, the Maps app brings up a version of Microsoft Bing Maps.

- **Messaging:** This app lets you send text messages to friends through Facebook, Microsoft's Instant Messenger, and other systems.

- **Music:** This app plays music stored on your computer. But Microsoft hopes you'll buy music from its store, as well.

- **News:** Visit here to read the news of the day, compiled from various news services.

- **People:** The beauty of the People app comes from its openness. After you enter your accounts — Facebook, Twitter, Google, and others — the People app grabs all your contacts, as well as their information, for easy access in other apps, such as Mail and Messaging.

- **Photos:** This app displays photos stored on your computer, as well as on accounts you may have on Facebook, Flickr, or SkyDrive.

- **Reader:** This handy app reads documents stored in the Adobe Portable Document Format (PDF). It jumps into action when you try to open any file stored in that format, whether from a website or an e-mail attachment.

- **SkyDrive:** This app provides access to Microsoft's cloud storage service, which lets you store files online for access from any computer, tablet, and smartphone that can access SkyDrive and for which you enter your SkyDrive credentials. It's similar to the popular Box, Dropbox, and Google Drive services.

- **Sports:** You can find sports news and scores here, as well as a way to add listings for your favorite sports teams.

- **Store:** The Windows Store is the only way to add more Start screen apps to your Start screen. (You can buy apps for the Windows Desktop in the usual ways, such as buying installation discs or downloads from application makers.)

- **Travel:** Resembling a travel agent's billboard, this app lists travel hot spots, complete with maps, panoramic photos, reviews, and links for booking flights and hotels.

- **Video:** This app provides a video rental store that you can use to download movies and TV shows from, but you can also play any videos you've added to your computer.

- **Weather:** This weather station forecasts a week's worth of weather in your area, but only if you grant it permission to access your location information. (Unless your computer has a GPS — Global Positioning System — the app narrows down your location by closest city rather than street address.)

Getting Apps from the Windows Store

The big change in Windows 8 is the introduction of the Start screen environment that runs that new breed of app optimized for touchscreens and simple, full-screen display on any device. There's only one place to get Start screen apps: the Windows Store, which you access using the Store app on the Start screen. (Sorry, but you can't buy Windows Desktop apps there.)

To access the Windows Store, you need to have a Microsoft account set up. If you signed in to your PC with a local account, a banner appears when you try to install or buy an app from the store, asking you to sign in with your Microsoft account. If you don't have a Microsoft account, you can create one from that banner.

When you enter the Windows Store, you see promoted apps in the Spotlight section, as well as tiles that open lists of apps: All Stars (most popular), Top Free, Rising Stars, and New Releases. If you scroll to the right, you'll see groups for various categories such as Games and Productivity. Sadly, there's no way to jump quickly to a desired category, but you can search within the Windows Store by using the Search charm — or just by typing a name in the app with a physical keyboard.

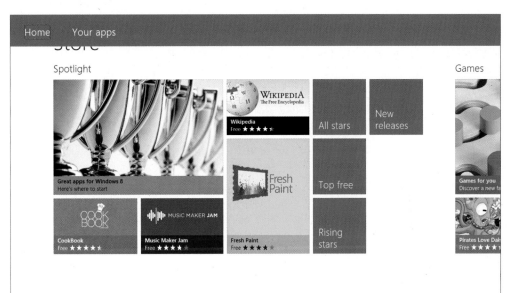

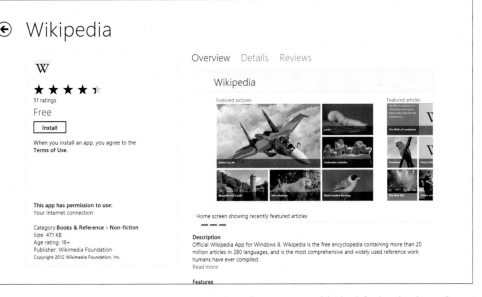

The Windows Store (top) and the details for the Wikipedia app (bottom)

In any category, tap an app to get more details on it. Each app has three panes you can switch among: Overview; Details (including any release notes, supported PC processors, and supported languages); and Reviews. To the left of these panes is a summary box with user ratings, an Install button, a list of permissions the app has on your PC's information, the app's size, the app developer, and its age rating.

TIP

If an app appears with a white background, you have already installed it. You also can see a list of apps purchased through your account by clicking or tapping Your Apps on the Control bar. You can install those apps you've purchased but haven't installed, or you can clear those you no longer want on the Store's App bar.

To buy apps, you need more than a Microsoft account: You need to give Microsoft your PayPal bill-payment account, if you have one, or credit card information to charge your purchases against (it's required even for free apps). When in the Store app, use the Settings charm to add or modify your payment options by clicking or tapping Accounts at the top and completing the relevant payment details.

REMEMBER

If you get an app and you don't want it, go to the Start screen and uninstall it by right-clicking its tile or, on a touchscreen PC, by dragging its tile to the bottom of the screen, to open the App bar. Then click or tap the Uninstall icon. The app is removed from all computers that are tied to the same Microsoft account.

The Settings charm for the Store app also provides the following controls specific to the app:

- **Your Account pane:** A list of PCs you've purchased apps from (you can install apps on as many as five PCs linked to your Microsoft account); you can remove those bought from a specific PC.

- **Preferences pane:** Options to favor apps in your preferred languages and to favor apps that include accessibility features.

- **App Updates:** Options to automatically update apps, check for updates, and force all purchased apps to sync to the current PC.

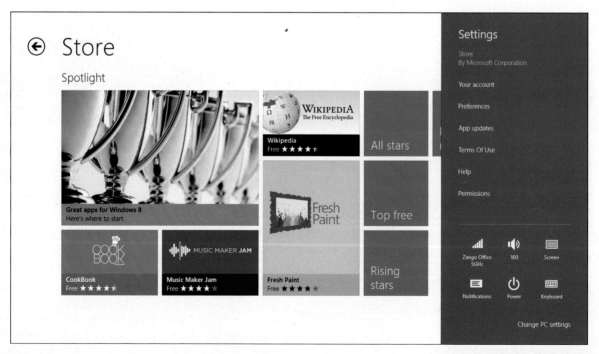

The Windows Store's Settings charm

DUMMIES

Working with Windows Desktop Apps

● *Finding and opening applications* ● *Introducing Windows 8–style apps*
● *The applications that come with the Windows Desktop*

The Start screen may make you work with apps in new ways, so the Windows Desktop may come as a relief: Its apps are the familiar Windows apps you've been running in Windows XP, Vista, and 7. You install them from CDs, DVDs, or downloaded installation files as you always have. And they have the familiar user interface from the earlier Windows versions.

If you've switched from Windows XP to Windows 8, note that the appearance of the windows, such as the title bar and menus, may have changed a little. Also, newer applications use the Ribbon interface below menus or instead of menus. But if you've used Windows 7, you'll see very few changes in Windows 8 when it comes to Windows Desktop apps — there's essentially no difference other than removing most 3D effects from application frames and buttons.

Accessing Applications

The biggest change in the Windows Desktop is the disappearance of the Start menu, which in previous versions of Windows provided easy access to your installed applications. To open applications in the Windows Desktop, you'll need to use one of these techniques instead:

✔ **Documents folder:** In File Explorer (formerly called Windows Explorer), navigate to your Documents folder or to a folder that contains a file you want to work with, and then double-click or double-tap it to open it in its application.

- **Program Files (x86) folder:** In File Explorer, navigate to the Program Files (x86) folder in the C: drive to see available applications, and then double-click or double-tap the desired application to open it.

- **Windows Desktop taskbar:** Pin running apps to the Windows Desktop taskbar so they remain available whenever you want to run them.

- **Start screen:** From the Start screen, open the App bar and click or tap All Apps. In the screen that appears, locate a Windows Desktop application, right-click it (or, on a touchscreen, drag it to the App bar and release it), and click or tap Pin to Start. This lets you launch the application without first switching to the Windows Desktop. (Some Windows Desktop apps automatically add their tiles to the Start screen when you install them, such as Google Chrome and Microsoft Office 2013.)

You press ▮+1, ▮+2, and ▮+3, respectively, to switch to the first, second, and third open apps on the Windows Desktop taskbar, respectively. You also can simply click or tap an app's icon on the taskbar to switch to it.

Many applications on the Windows Desktop don't automatically open the onscreen keyboard on a PC tablet when you tap a text field. To get the onscreen keyboard, tap the Keyboard icon in the taskbar.

Introducing Windows 8–Style Apps

The old, familiar Windows Desktop applications, such as Windows Media Player and Acrobat Reader, work essentially no differently in Windows 8 than in Windows 7. However, that's not necessarily true when it comes to new software designed for Windows 8, such as Microsoft Office 2013 (due for release in early 2013 but available in a preview version since summer 2012). These Windows 8–style applications run in full-screen mode by default. To get the toolbar, Ribbon bar, and other controls, you need to switch to the regular view you know and love from Windows 7.

To do that, click or tap the Exit Full Screen button (the ... icon) in the upper right of the screen. To go back to full-screen view, click or tap the Enter Full Screen button (the opening-window icon) at the top of the screen.

Exit Full Screen

Enter Full Screen

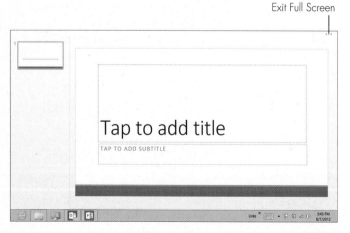
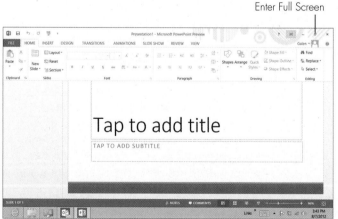

The full-screen view (left) and the regular view (right) for an example Windows 8–style app (PowerPoint 2013)

The Apps You Get with the Windows Desktop

Just as the Start screen comes with a selection of apps provided by Microsoft, so does the Windows Desktop. These applications should be familiar because they're the same set Microsoft has provided in other versions of Windows:

- **Calculator:** The name says it all!

- **Character Map:** A utility for inserting special symbols and foreign characters into your text.

- **Command Prompt:** A utility that lets you run DOS commands, an obsolete way of interacting with the PC that only IT people use today.

- **Internet Explorer 10 (IE 10):** Microsoft's web browser. Note that the Windows Desktop version supports Java and third-party plug-ins to extend its capabilities. (These plug-ins also can create security vulnerabilities, however.) The Start screen version includes Flash but doesn't let you add plug-ins.

- **Math Input Panel:** A floating dialog box where you can enter mathematical equations by drawing them and having the panel convert them to text that you can copy and paste into documents.

- **Notepad:** Microsoft's basic text editor, which can work with unformatted text files.

- **Paint:** A very basic program for editing photos and screen images.

- **Remote Desktop Connection:** A program that lets someone manage your PC from an Internet connection. In Windows 8 Pro and Windows Enterprise, it also lets you manage other PCs.

- **Snipping Tool:** A utility that lets you capture all or part of the Windows Desktop's screen as an image file (great for documentation and to show remote tech support what you're seeing onscreen). *Tip:* To capture the whole screen, whether you're on the Start screen or the Windows Desktop, press ⊞+PrtScr. On some keyboards, PrtScr may not be its own key — instead it may appear as a label on another key that requires you also press Fn, such as ⊞+Fn+Insert on a Samsung Slate PC tablet.

- **Sound Recorder:** A utility that records a sound file from the PC's internal or external microphone.

- **Steps Recorder:** A utility that records the actions you take in the Windows Desktop so you can play them back to automate tasks you do frequently. It essentially creates automated macros from your actions.

- **Sticky Notes:** An app that leaves virtual sticky notes on your desktop on which you can type reminders and other, er, notes.

- **Task Manager:** A utility that not only shows you what's running on your PC and how much resources those apps are taking, but also lets you force-quit applications that are not responding or that are getting in the way of other applications being able to run.

- **Windows Defender:** Microsoft's antivirus application.

- **Windows Media Player:** Microsoft's application to play music and video files.

- **WordPad:** A lightweight word processor that can do basic text formatting and work with Word and RTF (Rich Text Format) files.

- **XPS Viewer:** A utility that opens Microsoft's own XPS format, a sort-of competitor to Adobe's PDF.

TIP

The easiest way to get to these Windows Desktop applications is through the Start screen. Open the App bar and click or tap All Apps and then scroll through the apps to find them. They're scattered throughout the Windows Accessories and Windows System groups, and IE 10 is in the main applications group.

TIP

Many new PCs come with additional apps installed by the PC maker. Some are useful, but most aren't. If you go to a Microsoft store retail outlet, you can get PCs without such *junkware* added; these stores also offer a $100 service to remove such junkware from new PCs you bought elsewhere. Also, many PC sellers offer PCs that, for a relatively low price, add Microsoft Office.

Choosing between the Start Screen and Desktop

A consequence of Windows 8 having two parallel environments (the Start screen and Windows Desktop) loosely connected via the Start screen and the charms is that you often have two applications that do the same thing. For example, you can play videos in the Start screen via the Video app or in the Windows Desktop via the Windows Media Player application; music can likely be played in either the Music app or in Windows Media Player. (They all access the Videos and Music libraries in the Windows Desktop.) Likewise, there's the Start screen version of the Internet Explorer 10 browser and the Windows Desktop version.

If you install Microsoft Office — which nearly every PC has — you have two e-mail programs: Mail and Outlook. And if you use Adobe Reader or Acrobat in the Windows Desktop, you also have Windows Reader in the Start screen, which you can use to view PDF files.

That duality can be frustrating and can even cause some practical issues. For example, the Start screen's Mail app on a PC tablet often won't connect to corporate e-mail because corporate Exchange servers usually require mobile devices such as tablets to have encryption, which older PC tablets don't support. But that same unencrypted tablet is able to connect when you use Outlook instead on the Windows Desktop, because corporate servers see Windows Desktop as if it were any old PC, and thus make it exempt from the encryption requirement. (It makes no sense to require encryption on only some types of devices, but sadly this is a common setup in large businesses.)

The surest way to run the application you want is to launch it directly, either in the Start screen or Windows Desktop. But if you double-click a file in File Explorer or in an e-mail or other message, Windows 8 will open whatever app it has decided is the right one — including a Start screen app instead of the Windows Desktop app. For several file types, such as music, documents, image, and video files, Windows 8 asks the first time you double-click or double-tap a file of that type which app you want to use as the default.

You can change the defaults in three ways:

- **Via the Open With menu:** Right-click or tap and hold a file in File Explorer and choose Open With➜*filetype* from the contextual menu that appears, to choose which app should always open that type of file when it is double-clicked or double-tapped.

- **For an app in the Default Programs control panel:** Open the Default Programs control panel and click or tap Associate a File Type or Protocol with a Program. A list of file extensions and their default applications appears at left; select the one you whose default application you want to change, click or tap Change Program, and click or tap the new default app in the list that appears. Close the control panel when done.

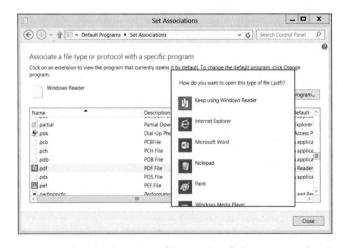

Change which app opens a file type in the Default Programs control panel.

- **For a file extension in the Default Programs control panel:** Open the Default Programs control panel and click or tap Set Your Program Defaults. A list of apps appears at left; select the one you want to be the default for *all* compatible files and click or tap Set This Program as Default. Close the control panel when you're done.

Working with Files

IN THIS ARTICLE

● *How applications access files* ● *Where files are stored* ● *Finding files*

Perhaps you've noticed that there are no files or folders on the Start screen. For example, when you snap a photo using the PC's camera in the Camera app, there's no folder displayed containing it. When you want to play music in the Music app or attach a file to an e-mail in Mail, you get a list of files, but you can't navigate to other folders or disks.

The Start screen and Windows Desktop may be separate environments, but one thing they share is the Windows file system — that is, the files and folders you know from File Explorer found on the Windows Desktop.

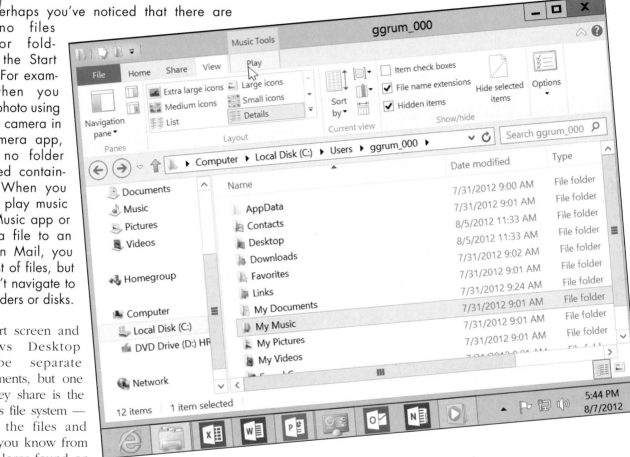

Start screen apps typically store and access files in predetermined folders, such as the My Music folder in the Libraries section of File Explorer for music files, the My Pictures folder for screen captures and photos taken with the PC's camera, and the My Videos folder for videos taken with the camera. (These folders, along with their public counterparts Public Music, Public Pictures, and Public Videos, comprise the Music, Pictures, and Videos libraries, respectively.)

Windows Desktop apps work with files as they have in previous versions of Windows, typically through the Open and Save As dialog boxes that can navigate through the PC's disks and folders. You access these dialog boxes from the File menu that appears at the top of most Windows apps.

TIP

Some applications designed for Windows Vista and 7 hide the menu bar that contains the File menu option and use icons instead on the toolbar or Ribbon. But they usually have an option to display the menus if you prefer: Press Alt to temporarily display the menu bar or choose Organize→Layout→Show Menu Bar from the toolbar to permanently display the menu bar in the current application.

The Basics of Files

Everything inside your computer is stored on a disk. Your computer has a primary disk, formally called the internal *hard disk.* You may see this disk referred to as the *C: drive;* Windows usually displays it as Local Disk (C:). (The terms *drive* and *disk* are interchangeable.)

When you save a document, you create a file on a disk. Many other files on the disk belong to the programs you use, including the thousands of files that make up Windows 8.

Disks are organized into *folders,* which are containers for files. Folders can hold folders, which are referred to as *subfolders.* Windows 8 comes set up with several folders to help you organize your files by type. For example, all your photos go into the Pictures folder, and all your documents go into the Documents folder. Windows stores these folders inside the Libraries folder, and it provides quick access to them in the Navigation pane — the left side of File Explorer.

If you start with the C: drive in File Explorer, you'll see several folders:

- ✔ **Windows,** which holds the components of Windows itself; you should leave this folder and its contents alone.

- ✔ **Program Files,** which holds Start screen apps, and **Program Files (x86)**, which holds Windows Desktop apps.

- ✔ **Users,** which holds a folder for every person who has an account on the PC, plus a folder named Public that is visible to all users of a PC and those connected to it via the network. Each person's files are stored inside their user folder. In each user folder are the folders most people think of as "their" folders:

  - *Desktop,* which stores anything displayed on the desktop.

  - *Downloads,* which is the default folder for browsers to save files to.

  - *Favorites,* which stores bookmarks for web pages used by Internet Explorer 10. You really shouldn't put other files here.

  - *My Documents,* which is where most applications want to save text, spreadsheet, presentation, and similar document files.

  - *My Music,* which is where music files are usually downloaded to or stored by the Music and Windows Media Player apps.

  - *My Pictures,* which is where pictures (such as photos and screen captures taken on the PC or downloaded from a music store or website) are saved.

  - *My Videos,* which is where movies (such as videos taken on the PC or downloaded from a video store or website) are saved.

- ✔ **Intel** and **PerfLogs** are folders that Windows uses for its own purposes. You should leave them alone.

Getting fast access to folders

Note that you get quick access to several of these folders in the Navigation pane on the left side of the File Explorer application window. In its Favorites section are quick links to Desktop and Downloads, as well as to Recent Places, which opens a list of recently used folders. In its Libraries section are quick links to the My Documents, My Music, My Pictures, and My Videos folders, though the word *My* is omitted in those links. If you have multiple disks, including thumb drives and DVDs, attached to your PC, they appear in the Computer section. The Homegroup link takes you to your personal network's storage, whereas the Network link connects you to all available network resources.

Here are the actions you can do with folders:

- ✔ **To add folders to the Start screen:** In File Explorer, right-click or tap and hold a folder and choose Pin to Start from its contextual menu. A tile for that folder appears on the Start screen, and you can double-click or double-tap it there to open it in File Explorer. (To remove it from the Start screen, open its App bar and then click or tap Unpin from Start. This does *not* delete the folder.)

- ✔ **To add a folder to the Favorites list in File Explorer's Navigation pane:** Open the desired folder, right-click or tap and hold on Favorites in the Navigation pane, and choose Add Current Location to Favorites. (To remove it from the Favorites list, right-click or tap and hold on the folder name in that list and choose Remove. Again, this does *not* delete the folder.)

Selecting folders and files

To select a folder or file so you can manipulate it, click or tap it. To select multiple files, click or tap the first item in the list and then hold Shift and click or tap the last item to select all items between them. Or, if you're using a touchscreen, use check boxes to select multiple files, even if they aren't adjacent. The ability to use check boxes is enabled by default on a touchscreen PC but not on a regular PC.

If you're using a mouse, follow these steps to use check boxes to select files; touchscreen users can skip to Step 3 because check box selection is already enabled:

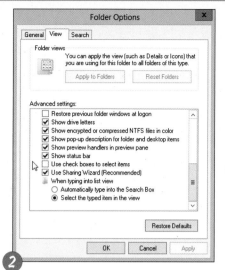

1 In File Explorer, enable check box selection by going to the Ribbon's View tab and clicking or tapping the Options button.

2 In the Folder Options dialog box that appears, go to the View tab and scroll through the options until you find Use Check Boxes to Select Items and then select that check box. Click or tap the OK button.

3 Select the first file by clicking or tapping the area to the left of its filename. (You won't see the check box until you select it with a click or a tap or until you hover over it with the mouse pointer.) Repeat this action to select more files. (To deselect a file, select the check box again to remove the check mark.)

The Ribbon's Home tab in File Explorer offers other methods for selecting files and folders: The *Select All* option does just what it says — selects all objects in a folder or library. *Select None* works similarly. And *Invert Selection* switches the selection, selecting what hadn't been selected and deselecting what had been selected.

Creating and renaming folders and files

You can create your own folders both within these folders and on the C: drive. You can create a new folder in several ways:

- Right-click or tap and hold in an empty area of a disk's or folder's file list and choose New➜Folder from the contextual menu.

- Click the New Folder icon above the menu bar in File Explorer.

- Click the New Folder icon on the Ribbon's Home tab.

- Press Ctrl+Shift+N.

To create a file, the easiest way is to create a new document in an application and save it.

In File Explorer, you also can right-click or tap and hold an empty area of the file list and choose New➜Folder from the contextual menu. You get a blank document that you can open in a compatible application.

To rename a file or folder, click or tap it, wait a second, and click it again. Its name becomes highlighted; just type in a new name and click elsewhere on the screen when you're done.

Moving and copying folders and files

You can move files and folders in several ways, but most are too much work. The two simplest ways are as follows:

- Drag a file or folder from its folder over a folder in the Navigation pane of File Explorer; if that folder has subfolders, they'll appear if you hover a few seconds. When the desired folder appears in the Navigation pane, release the mouse button or your finger to drop the item to its new location.

- Select the file or folder and press Ctrl+X to cut it, navigate to the desired new location in File Explorer, and press Ctrl+V to paste the cut file, in essence moving it.

TIP

You also can usually create folders in the Save As dialog box when saving files from Windows Desktop apps; click the New Folder button (an icon of a folder with a plus sign).

You can also open an existing document and save it with a new name, making a copy that you then modify. Alternatively, you can select a file or folder, press Ctrl+C, navigate to a different location in File Explorer, and press Ctrl+V to paste a copy of that item.

Deleting folders and files

If you want to trash a file or folder, freeing up the bits it takes on the disks for use by other files and folders, you have several easy options to do so:

- Drag the file or folder into the Recycle Bin on the desktop.
- Select the file or folder and press Ctrl+D.
- Select the file or folder, and in the Home tab of the File Explorer's Ribbon, click the Delete icon.
- Select the file or folder and right-click or tap and hold the item, and then choose Delete from the contextual menu that appears.

Searching for Files

The easiest way to find a file in Windows 8 is to use the Search charm and make sure that Files is active. (Click or tap the Files icon to make it active.) Then enter your search term in the text field and press Enter or click or tap the Search button (the magnifying-glass icon). A list of matching files appears in the pane at left.

You can also search in the Windows Desktop by using the traditional method. But truth be told, it's not as easy to search the old way as it is in the Search charm. But if you prefer to work in the familiar Windows Desktop, open File Explorer and click or tap Computer in the Navigation pane at left. This is important because File Explorer usually starts its search from whatever folder you or the last application was most recently using, which means it won't search the entire PC. If you start at Computer, you're sure to search everything the PC can see. Type your search term in the search field below the Ribbon and then press Enter or click or tap the magnifying-glass icon. A list of matching files appears below.

The File Explorer approach does have a couple advantages: You can navigate the folder hierarchy to narrow your search, and you can change the way the files display using the Ribbon's View tab options, such as the icon size or as a simple list.

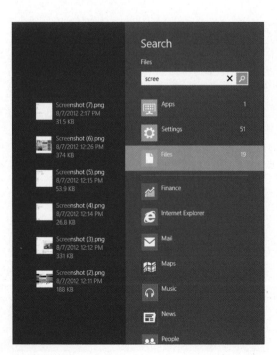

The Search charm and its search results (left) and searching in File Explorer (right)

DUMMIES

Files in the Cloud with SkyDrive

One of the beauties of using a Microsoft account is that you can link as many as five PCs to that account and have their settings and apps automatically update over the Internet, so they stay in sync with each other. But any *files* you store on a PC do not sync to the others, so if you start working on something on your work PC but forget to copy it to your PC tablet, it won't be there when you turn on that PC tablet at your hotel.

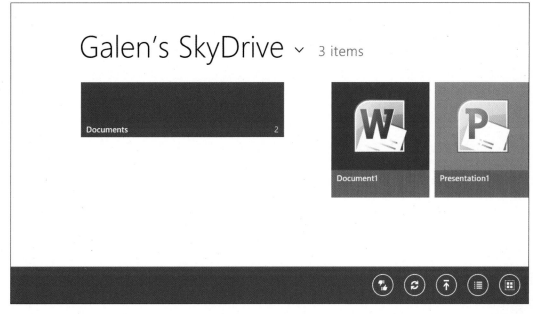

Unless you use SkyDrive, that is.

SkyDrive is Microsoft's cloud storage service, storing files on Microsoft's servers and making them available via an Internet connection. The concept is not new: Google Drive (formerly Google Docs), Dropbox, and Box have offered a similar service for years. All of them, including SkyDrive, give you some storage for free (usually 2GB to 5GB, but 7GB for SkyDrive) and charge an annual fee for additional storage capacity.

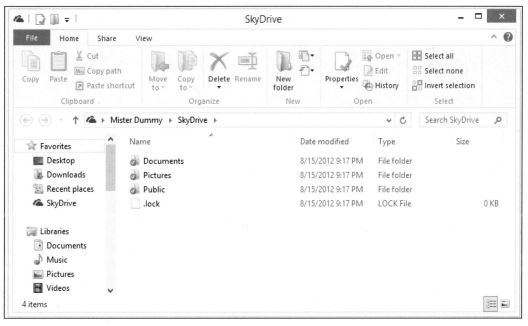

SkyDrive on the Start screen (top) and the Windows Desktop's File Explorer (bottom)

What's different about SkyDrive is that it comes preinstalled in Windows 8, and some apps such as Office 2013 can access it directly for working on files in its Open and Save As dialog boxes, rather than make you navigate to its files as with competing services. Microsoft wants you to use SkyDrive, so it has tilted the playing field in SkyDrive's favor.

To use SkyDrive in the Start screen, just run the SkyDrive app from the Start screen. On the Windows Desktop, you have to download the SkyDrive application from **www. skydrive.com**; after you do so, you can access SkyDrive in File Explorer by looking in the Navigation pane's Favorites section.

When you open SkyDrive in either environment and you aren't already signed in to SkyDrive, you're asked to sign in (you can use your Microsoft account, Live ID, or SkyDrive login) or create an account.

By default, your SkyDrive account usually has three folders — Documents, Pictures, and Public — but it could have just Documents.

TIP

SkyDrive is also available for Windows Vista and 7; Windows Phone; Mac OS X Lion and later; Android (used by various smartphones and tablets); and iOS (used by the iPhone, iPad, and iPod touch); as well as via the web for other operating systems. You can download it from **www.skydrive.com** or get it from the Apple App Store for iOS, the Google Play store for Android, or the Windows Store for Windows Phone. Thus, you can share files across multiple types of computers, not just with Windows 8 PCs.

Working with SkyDrive on the Windows Desktop

You can easily navigate to SkyDrive in File Explorer from the Navigation pane as if it were a local folder or disk, adding and removing folders and files using the standard File Explorer methods.

Likewise, you navigate to it in apps through Open and Save As dialog boxes as if it were a local disk or folder.

SkyDrive displays notifications in the taskbar when files are updated on SkyDrive, and you can make the SkyDrive icon visible so you have easy access to its settings when desired. To do so, click or tap the up-pointing triangle icon in the icon tray to get a list of hidden icons and to get the Customize option that lets you change what displays in the icon tray. To have the SkyDrive icon appear, scroll through the icons list and choose Show Icon and Notifications in the menu adjacent to SkyDrive.

Working with SkyDrive in the Start Screen

The SkyDrive app on the Start screen works very differently and does less than the SkyDrive app on the Windows Desktop. For example, you can't create or move files. But you can add or delete folders, and upload files to it.

To open a file from the Start screen's SkyDrive, click or tap it. The file will open in the default application for that file type, whether a Start screen app or a Windows Desktop app.

To delete a file stored in SkyDrive from the Start screen's SkyDrive, right-click it or, on a touchscreen PC, drag it down toward the bottom of the screen, to open the App bar. Then click or tap the Delete icon on the App bar.

Use the App bar to delete files in SkyDrive

FOR DUMMIES

To download a file from SkyDrive to your PC, you need to open the file and save it locally from the app it opened. Here's how to add files from your PC to SkyDrive via the Start screen SkyDrive app:

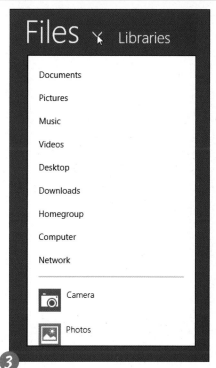

1 In the main SkyDrive screen, open the App bar and click or tap the Upload icon.

2 The screen that appears displays any documents on your PC in the current folder (such as Pictures, which displays the contents of the PC's My Pictures folder). Any folders appear as tiles; click or tap the tile to see its files. Click or tap Go Up to move up to the parent folder.

3 To switch to a different folder on your PC, tap the ∨ icon to the right of Files to open a menu of folders and then tap the desired folder to see its files.

4 Select the files you want to add to SkyDrive. Simply click or tap each file; click a selected file to deselect it. (Click the Select All icon in the App bar to select all files.) Then click the Add to SkyDrive button.

TIP

Click or tap the Details icon on the App bar to see files organized as a list with information such as file size. The icon becomes the Thumbnails icon; click or tap it to view the files as tiles. (It then becomes the Details icon again.)

Fetching Files from Another PC

SkyDrive has a cool feature called *fetching* that lets it access files on another Windows PC, such as to get that file you forgot on your PC but need at a client site where you have just your PC tablet (or iPad, iPhone, MacBook, Windows Phone, Android device, or other supported device). The trick is that the Windows PC with the files you want has to be turned on and signed in to your Microsoft (or SkyDrive) account, with the fetching feature enabled. The SkyDrive Fetch feature lets you go into any PC (but not Macs or other devices) that's signed in with your Microsoft account and retrieve files from that computer.

When you set up SkyDrive on the Windows Desktop, by default the Make Files on This PC Available to Me on My Other Devices option was selected, which means fetching was enabled. If you deselected it, you can enable fetching from the Windows Desktop taskbar (not from the Settings charm for the Start screen SkyDrive app) by right-clicking or tapping and holding the SkyDrive icon and choosing Settings from the contextual menu; then select the Make Files on This PC Available to Me on My Other Devices option and click or tap OK. (If you're using a corporate PC, your IT department may have disabled fetching, in which case you can't turn it on.)

When fetching is enabled, here's how it works:

1 With your browser, go to **www.skydrive.com** and sign in using your Microsoft or SkyDrive account.

2 At the lower left of the SkyDrive window is the PCs list, with the names of any signed-in PCs available. Click a computer's name to open it.

3 Your files display. Click or tap a folder to open its contents.

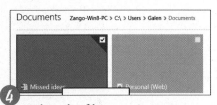

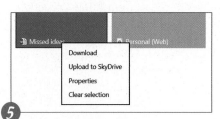

4 Select the files you want to copy to SkyDrive; check marks appear to their left (if you are using the tiles, the check marks appear at the upper right of the tiles).

5 In the Windows Desktop, click or tap the desired action: Open, Download, or Copy to SkyDrive. In the Start screen, choose Download or Upload to SkyDrive from the contextual menu that appears.

The first time you access a computer this way, you're asked to enter a security code to verify you're permitted to access that computer's files. When you signed up for SkyDrive, you were asked for a phone number to use for verification; the code is usually texted to that phone, or a voicemail is left with the code. If you didn't get the code, click or tap I Didn't Get the Code and then choose a phone number or e-mail address to send the code to from the pop-up menu. (You can't add new numbers or addresses here; you must update your Microsoft or Windows Live account's security settings to do so.)

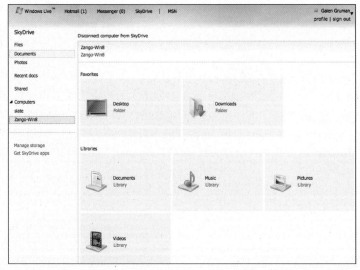

DUMMIES

Surfing the Web

IN THIS ARTICLE

● *Connecting wirelessly to the Internet* ● *Using Internet Explorer 10 on the Start screen*
● *Working with IE 10 on the Windows Desktop*

Windows 8 really likes the Internet, and it assumes you have an Internet connection when you install and run it. It checks to see whether you're connected to the Internet via a cable modem, dial-up modem, or DSL modem, whether over a wired Ethernet cable or via a Wi-Fi wireless connection. It always shows the connection status on its lock screen, as well as in the Settings charm. Windows 8 also regularly uses the Internet to check for and download updates and to give you access to the web. With an Internet connection and a Microsoft account, Windows 8 even syncs the settings and Start screen apps across as many as five PCs signed into that same account.

You can, of course, use Windows 8 without an Internet connection, but you won't get the full experience. (You can find out more about connecting wirelessly and networking computers later in this book.)

Internet Explorer 10 in the Start screen environment (top) and on the Windows Desktop (bottom)

Comparing the Two Versions of IE 10

Windows 8 provides two versions of Internet Explorer 10 (IE 10), one on the Windows Desktop and one on the Start screen. Because these browsers are basically the same beast, they share your browsing history, cookies, saved passwords, and temporary files. Deleting those items from one version of the browser also deletes them from the other.

The browsers differ in a few ways, but most obviously through the limitations of the Start screen browser:

- It shows sites only in full-screen view; you can't place two sites side by side to compare them.

- It doesn't let you set a Home screen. Instead, the browser always opens to the last site you visited.

- It can display Flash content only on Microsoft-approved websites, so on some sites you'll miss out on some movies and advertisements (not that you'll miss the ads!).

- It can't run plug-ins such Adobe AIR or Adobe Reader.

You might consider using a competing browser such as Firefox (**www.getfirefox.com**), Safari (**www.apple.com/safari**), or Chrome (**www.google.com/chrome**). All three support many more HTML5 capabilities than IE 10, which means on more advanced websites you can do more with videos, animations, and interactive elements — all aspects of the emerging HTML5 web standard. And remember: You can use more than one browser in Windows, so it's not an either/or choice.

On a touchscreen, double-tap the screen to zoom in to the web page. Double-tap again to zoom back out. You can also use the pinch and expand gestures to zoom in and out to the degree you prefer. These techniques work in both versions of IE 10.

Getting online in the first place

Most people in North America, Europe, and other developed countries already have Internet connections set up. Many use broadband connections from a cable company or phone company, and some use wireless broadband services when running wires to their (usually rural) homes is difficult. And a shrinking but still large group uses their phone lines and a device called a dial-up modem that lets it connect to the Internet, though very slowly. Many people also connect to the Internet when they're on the road via Wi-Fi networks, such as at cafés, hotels, and even parks; some of these are free, but others require a subscription or an account with a broadband provider.

Here are some options depending on where you're establishing a connection:

- **Home:** If you don't have an Internet connection, your choices are usually governed by where you live. In urban and suburban areas, you typically can subscribe to a service from a cable TV provider or phone company (DSL or fiber-optic). To the cable, phone, or other line that comes into your house, you connect a device called a *modem* that acts as the way station between your computers and other devices and the provider's Internet service. That modem may have Ethernet jacks to plug computers and devices into and/or it may provide a Wi-Fi network your devices can connect to wirelessly, so you can share that connection with multiple computers and mobile devices. Or you may need to connect a router to that modem to gain the Ethernet and Wi-Fi connections; your provider — called an *Internet service provider* (ISP) — will tell you what you need to use its service and often will sell or rent you the equipment.

- **Work:** At work, businesses use similar technologies and provide an Ethernet connection or sign-in information for Wi-Fi access.

- **On the road:** When you're on the road, you can look for a Wi-Fi hot spot and connect. In some cases, you pay an hourly or daily fee to use that hot spot. Your ISP may also have a relationship with some hot spots that lets you access them for free by entering a username and password that the ISP provides you. You typically enter that information after connecting to the hot spot; your browser may open automatically and present a sign-in screen, but if not, open your browser and then try to open any website to get the sign-in screen to appear.

Using IE 10 on the Start Screen

Built for on-the-fly browsing, the Start screen's browser works quickly. Unlike most Start screen apps, the IE 10 App bar displays by default, so you can immediately enter a web address in the address field and access the basic controls. After you type in a web address, press Enter or tap the right-arrow icon to the right of the field to have IE 10 open it.

Note that, on a touchscreen, when you enter a web address, a set of tiles appears above the keyboard, showing frequently accessed web pages; click or tap one to open it. (You can't modify what appears in those tiles or change their order.)

TIP

If you're using the Start screen version of IE 10 and find yourself needing a more powerful browser, open the App bar (by right-clicking or, on a touchscreen, swiping up from the bottom edge or down from the top edge). Then click or tap the Page Tools icon (it looks like a wrench), and choose View in Desktop to switch to the Windows Desktop version of IE 10.

Tiles for frequently used web pages appear when you enter a web address

Control bar's thumbnails of recently viewed web pages

Tab Tools

New Tab

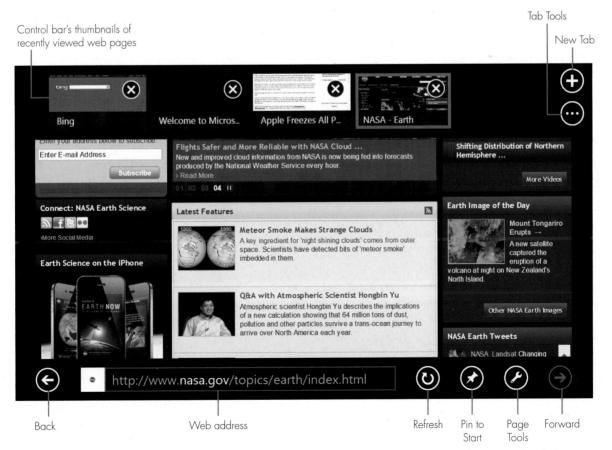

Back   Web address   Refresh   Pin to Start   Page Tools   Forward

The IE 10 controls on the Start screen

To see the Control bar, which shows thumbnails of the most recently visited web pages for easy access to them, right-click or, on a touchscreen, swipe up from the bottom edge or down from the top edge. (To hide both the App bar and Control bar, repeat the action.) You can delete web pages from the Control bar by clicking or tapping the Close (X) icon near its upper-right corner.

Touring the IE 10 controls

Here's what the IE 10 App bar and other onscreen controls in the Start screen do:

- **New Tab:** Opens a blank IE 10 screen with an address field along the bottom. Enter the address of the website you'd like to visit.

- **Back:** Revisit the page you visited just prior to this page. On a touchscreen, swipe to the left to go back to the previous page in your current session's browsing history.

- **Forward:** This lets you return to the page you just left. On a touchscreen, swipe to the left to go back to the previous page in your current session's browsing history.

- **Refresh:** This reloads the current page, gathering the latest content available.

- **Pin to Start:** This icon adds the page to your Start screen as a tile, giving you one-click access for a return visit.

- **Page Tools:** This opens a menu with three options: *Find on Page* lets you search for text on the current page, *View on Desktop* opens the page in IE 10 on the Windows Desktop, and *Get App for This Site* downloads an app to use to access the website's content. (If the Get App for This Site option is in gray, no such app is available.)

- **Tab Tools:** This opens a menu with two options: New InPrivate Tab and Close Tabs. The *New InPrivate Tab* option opens a new tab for visiting a website privately; the browser conveniently forgets you've visited that site, so someone else can't retrace your steps. The *Close Tabs* option removes the thumbnails of your previously viewed sites from the Control bar.

Saving text and images from a website

Often when you're visiting a website, you want to copy text or images from it.

To save just some of a web page's text when using a keyboard and mouse, select the text you want to grab, right-click it, and choose Copy from the contextual menu — or just select the text and press Ctrl+C. On a touchscreen, tap on the text, which causes the word where you tapped to be highlighted and for two circular handles to appear. Drag

those handles to determine the selection area; then tap and hold on one of those selection handles and choose Copy from the contextual menu that appears.

Open your word processor or other application and paste the text into a document. The easiest way to paste is to press Ctrl+V; on a touchscreen, tap into a text field or text-capable app, and then when the selection handle appears, tap it and choose Paste from the contextual menu.

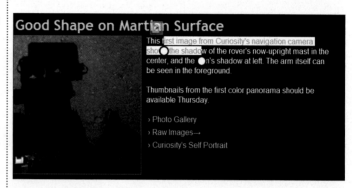

The selection handles that appear when selecting text on a touchscreen

When you browse through web pages and spot a picture that's too good to pass up, you can save it to your computer: Right-click or tap and hold the picture and choose Copy or Save to Picture Library from the contextual menu that appears.

- If you choose Paste, you can copy the image into a compatible application by using its Paste button or the keyboard shortcut Ctrl+V.

- If you choose Save to Picture Library, the image is saved to the My Pictures folder, which you typically access in the File Explorer in the Windows Desktop but can also be accessed in Start screen apps that allow for file navigation.

Don't use downloaded images for material you distribute or publish to others without permission. To use the image, you need to have permission from the copyright holder or ensure that it is not copyrighted (such as for NASA photos).

You search for websites using the Search charm when IE 10 is open. It searches only via the Bing search engine. If you want to use a different search engine, such as Google or Yahoo!, you need to go that search engine's website in IE 10 and use its web page to conduct your search.

Using IE 10 on the Windows Desktop

When you need more power than the Start screen's simplified browser has to offer, the full version of Internet Explorer 10 awaits you on the Windows Desktop. If you've used a PC, you almost certainly have used Internet Explorer before, though probably an earlier version. IE 10 works very much like recent Internet Explorer versions, especially those in Windows 7, so it shouldn't be much of an adjustment to use IE 10 on the Windows Desktop.

Touring IE 10's controls

Many of the core controls in IE 10 for the Windows Desktop work the same way they do in IE 10 for the Start screen — or in any browser, for that matter, including the Back,

Forward, Refresh, and New Tab buttons. Others are familiar from other previous editions of Internet Explorer and other browsers, such as:

- **Home:** This brings you to the web page you've designated as your home page or to a menu of several such pages. You can set your home page(s) by right-clicking or tapping and holding the Home button and choosing Add or Change Home Page from the contextual menu that appears. ***Note:*** The shortcut Alt+Home also opens the home page.

- **Search:** This lets you search the web for whatever text you enter. To add other search engines beyond the default Bing, click Add at the bottom of the Search pane. ***Note:*** The shortcut Ctrl+E also opens the Search pane.

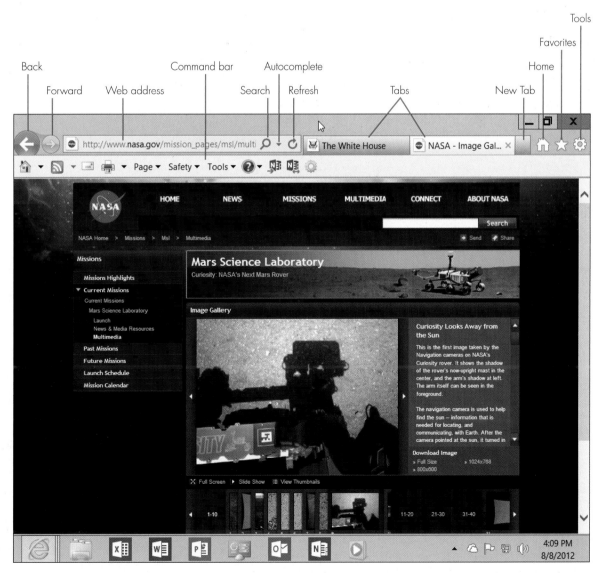

IE 10's controls in the Windows Desktop

✓ **Autocomplete:** As soon as you enter just a few characters, Internet Explorer opens a list of sites it "thinks" may be what you want to visit. Click or tap a site to revisit it; remove an unwanted site by hovering the pointer over it and then clicking the X icon that appears to the right of its name. (On a touchscreen, swipe from just above the site's name and release just below to display the X icon.)

✓ **Favorites:** This opens the Favorites list, a list of links that often lead to your favorite websites. From the Favorites list, you can click or tap the Add to Favorites button to add your currently viewed site to the list. *Note:* The shortcut Alt+C also opens the Favorites list.

✓ **Tools:** This opens a menu that's chock-full of Internet Explorer settings and commands, including Print, Zoom, and File (for saving the web page to your PC and searching within the web page). Use the Safety option to delete your browsing history, browse in private (handy for bank sites), or check suspicious websites for danger. *Note:* The shortcut Ctrl+T also opens the Tools menu.

IE 10 normally lives within the confines of its own application window. But occasionally it swells up to fill the entire screen, neatly trimming away both your menus and the desktop's taskbar. Full-screen mode looks great for movies, but the lack of menus leaves you with no way to switch to a different program. Well, there is a way: Just move the mouse to the top of the screen to display a toolbar. (On a touchscreen PC, that toolbar always displays when IE 10 is in full-screen mode.) A related tip: Press F11 to toggle in and out of full-screen mode.

Using the Command bar

Not shown by default in IE 10 is the Command bar, but it's handy to have available. To turn it on, right-click or tap and hold in the empty area above the toolbar and choose Command Bar in the contextual menu that appears. The Command bar duplicates many of the File, Safety, and other options on the Tools menu, but it adds several others:

✓ **Send web content via e-mail:** Choose Page➔Send Page by E-Mail to send an image of the current page to someone via e-mail, or choose Page➔Send Link by E-Mail to send just the web address.

✓ **Update Windows:** Choose Safety➔Windows Update to check for updates to Windows.

✓ **Adjust IE 10 settings:** Choose Tools➔Internet Options to open the Internet Options dialog box, where you can change settings for many aspects of IE 10's behavior. For example, you can set its level of trust for suspicious websites, determine whether browser history gets cleared every time you close the browser, manage browser plug-ins (called *add-ons* in the dialog box), and control how text, links, and images display.

IE 10 on the Windows Desktop provides two ways to make web pages accessible even when IE 10 isn't open. One way is to open the web page you want and then choose Tools➔Pin to Start in IE 10, which adds the current web page to the Start screen as a tile. The other way is to drag the site's icon to the left of its web address onto the Windows Desktop's taskbar to pin it there.

If you think you've messed up the Desktop's Internet Explorer beyond repair from adjusting various settings, relax. When all seems lost, you can return the program to its original settings with this trick: Choose Tools➔Internet Options, go to the Advanced pane, and click Reset. This action wipes out all of your settings, including your list of favorite sites, but it also removes any evil that may have been done to your browser.

Internet Explorer's secret history of your web visits

Internet Explorer keeps a record of every website you visit. Although Internet Explorer's History list provides a handy record of your computing activities, it's also a spy's dream. Here's how to manage the History list:

- **To keep tabs on what Internet Explorer is recording**: Click or tap the Favorites button and go to the History pane. Internet Explorer lists every website you've visited in the past 20 days. Feel free to sort the entries by clicking or tapping the little arrow to the right of the word *History.* You can sort them by date, alphabetically, most visited, or by the order you've visited on that particular day — a handy way to jump back to that site you found interesting this morning.

- **To delete a single entry from the history:** Right-click it or tap and hold it and choose Delete from the contextual menu. To delete the entire list, exit the Favorites list, press Ctrl+Shift+Del. You can also choose Tools➪Internet Options, and then click the Delete button in the Browsing History section. Either way, a menu appears, letting you delete your history and other items.

- **To turn off the history:** Click the Settings button instead of the Delete button. Then in the History section, change the Days to Keep Pages in History option to 0.

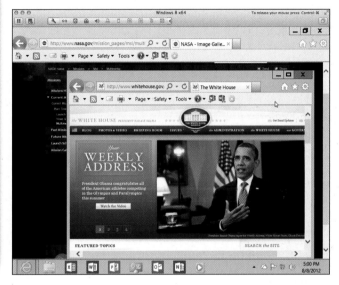

Dragging a browser tab into its own window

Working with browser tabs

Each time you open a browser tab, it gets added to the toolbar, next to the other open tabs. Click a tab to switch to it and click its Close button (the X icon) to close that tab completely.

But sometimes you want to see several web pages at the same time onscreen. To do that, you can detach a tab from the toolbar: Just drag the visible part of the tab in the toolbar out of the toolbar, and IE 10 creates a new window for that tab, which you can place anywhere you prefer onscreen. To put a tab back in with the others, drag its title back into the toolbar between or next to the tabs there. That's it!

Saving text and images from a website

You save a text selection in the Windows Desktop version of IE 10 the same way you do in the Start screen version: Select the text you want to grab, right-click it, and choose Copy from the contextual menu; or just select the text and press Ctrl+C. On a touchscreen, tap on the text, which causes the word where you tapped to be highlighted and for two circular handles to appear. Drag those handles to determine the selection area; then tap and hold on one of those selection handles and choose Copy from the contextual menu that appears.

In your word processor or other application, paste the text into a document. The easiest way to paste is to press Ctrl+V; on a touchscreen, tap into a text field or text-capable app, and then when the selection handle appears, tap it and choose Paste from the contextual menu that appears.

To save a picture from a website to your PC, right-click or tap and hold the picture and choose Save Picture As from the contextual menu that appears. In the Save Picture dialog box that appears, choose a new filename or stick with the filename used by the web page, and then click or tap Save to place your pilfered picture in your My Pictures folder. Just remember: Don't republish or share images you don't have permission to use.

Saving an image from a website in IE 10 for Windows Desktop

Downloading a program, song, or other file

Sometimes downloading is as easy as clicking a website's Download button. When the website asks where to save the file, choose your Downloads folder for easy retrieval. The file usually arrives within a few seconds. But when a website lacks a Download button, you need to take a few extra steps:

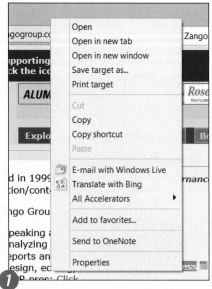

1 Right-click or tap and hold the link or button pointing to your desired file and choose Save Target As in the contextual menu that appears.

2 If you selected an application, Windows asks whether you want to run or save the file (so you can run it later). Click or tap Save, so you have the file on your computer for use later.

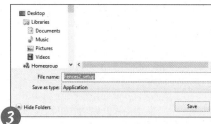

3 Navigate to your Downloads folder or wherever you want to save it, if necessary, and click the Save button.

No matter what type of file you're downloading, Windows 8 begins copying the file from the website to your hard disk. A window appears to tell you when it finishes downloading, and you can click or tap the Open Folder button to open the folder harboring your downloaded file.

 Many downloaded files come packaged in a tidy folder with a zipper on it, known as a *Zip file.* Windows 8 treats them like normal folders; just double-click or double-tap them to see inside them. To extract copies of the zipped files, right-click or tap and hold the zipped file and choose Extract All.

Working with plug-ins

Most browsers can do much more than display web pages, thanks to something called *plug-ins,* or *add-ons.* These are programs that can run from inside a browser to, for example, play movies, view PDF files, or run programs. The most commonly used ones are Adobe Flash, Adobe AIR, Adobe Reader, Apple QuickTime, Microsoft Silverlight, and Oracle Java.

Plug-ins are very handy, but they come at a cost: Some hackers use them to sneak past your PC's native defenses. And some websites lie about the plug-in they're installing, putting viruses or worse on your PC. (File-sharing sites and sites advertised to you in unsolicited e-mails are most likely to do so.) So if Internet Explorer says it needs a plug-in or the latest version of the software, click the Install or Yes button *only if you trust the website and the plug-in.*

TIP

If you accidentally install a plug-in, you can disable it. Choose Tools→Internet Options from the Command bar, go to the Programs pane, click the Manage Add-Ons button, scroll through the list of plug-ins, right-click or tap and hold the suspect one, and choose Disable from the contextual menu.

Connecting with E-Mail

1f you're under 30, you may wonder what e-mail is. Just kidding! But it's true that e-mail is less popular with younger people. That may explain why Microsoft has built just minimal e-mail capabilities into Windows 8: It has only the basic Mail app in the Start screen environment, and the Windows Desktop doesn't include a mail application.

Still, e-mail is a versatile, highly useful way to communicate, especially when you want to include detailed information and file attachments and be able to refer back to and even sort old e-mails — all activities that are either impossible or difficult to do in the instant-messaging services and social networking services that are so popular. Of course, it's not an either/or proposition: Most people can and should use all these communication channels

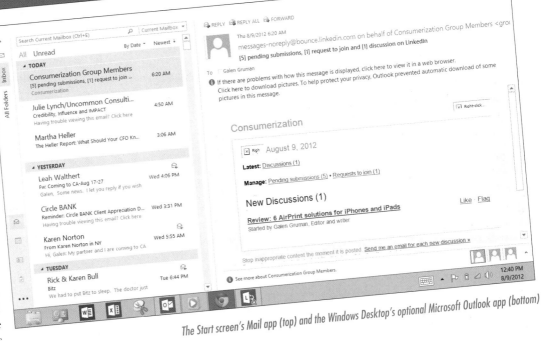

as appropriate for what they're trying to communicate and who they're trying to communicate with.

The Start screen's Mail app (top) and the Windows Desktop's optional Microsoft Outlook app (bottom)

Using Mail in the Start Screen

Click or tap the Mail tile in the Start screen environment to open the Mail app. Easy, right? Yes, but all you get is a blank screen with *Mail* at the upper left.

Setting up e-mail accounts

To really use mail, you first have to set up your e-mail accounts in Mail. To do so, open Mail and follow these steps:

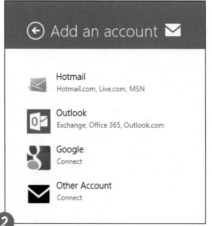

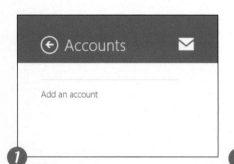

1 Open the Settings charm and click or tap Accounts in the Settings section.

2 On the screen that appears, click or tap Add an Account and then choose the type of e-mail account from the list that appears: Hotmail (including Outlook.com), Google, Outlook (Microsoft Exchange or Office 365), or Other Account. Choose the Other Account option if you use a POP or IMAP account — such as for the e-mail address provided by your Internet service provider, if you use a different service (such as yahoo.com or icloud.com), or if you have your own domain (such as wiley.com).

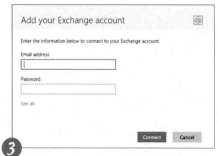

3 Enter your e-mail address and password on the screen that appears. If your e-mail has special settings (ask your IT department), tap or click See All to enter them. Then click or tap Connect, and Mail will try to connect to the e-mail server and set up the account on your PC. If it needs more information (typically for an Exchange account), a screen appears requesting it.

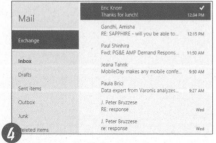

4 Your e-mail account is now ready and will begin downloading e-mail to your PC. To add another account, repeat Steps 1 through 3.

The Start screen's Mail does not support the most widely used type of e-mail account, known as POP (Post Office Protocol). You'll get an error message if you try to set up such an account.

FOR DUMMIES

Writing new e-mails

To compose an e-mail, click the New E-Mail button (the big + icon). Then fill in the following information:

- **Recipients:** At the left side, you enter the recipients in the To and Cc fields; type in addressees' e-mail addresses separated by commas or type in their names to have Mail look up possible matches from your address book; then click or tap the desired person from the list that appears.

  Also on the left side are one or two options, depending on whether you have multiple accounts set up:

  From Account, represented by the ∨ icon to the right of the current e-mail account. Click or tap it to open a menu that lets you change which e-mail account the message is sent from.

  Show More, which if clicked or tapped opens the Bcc field (to copy people secretly on the message) and Priority (to mark the message as high, normal, or low priority).

- **Subject:** On the right side of the screen, click or tap the Add a Subject placeholder text to enter a subject line for your e-mail. Then click or tap in the area below the line to enter your message.

- **Message:** You can do more than just type text in your message, because Mail also provides formatting and editing controls. To access them, be sure that text is selected or that the pointer is at least inside the text area; then open the App bar. If any text is selected, you'll see the Copy/Paste icon at the far left; click or tap it to get the Copy and Paste menu options. (If no text is selected, the icon becomes Paste and

has no menu.) You can also use the Ctrl+C and Ctrl+V keyboard shortcuts to copy and paste, of course.

At the right side of the App bar are the formatting controls:

Font: The options are Arial, Calibri, Cambria, Consolas, Georgia, Tahoma, Times New Roman, and Verdana, plus you can change the text size.

Bold, Italic, and Underline: These controls do exactly what you'd expect them to.

Text Color: You get ten swatches to choose from.

Highlight: This lets you color the background behind text. There are nine color options plus None to remove the highlighting.

Emoticons: This lets you insert smiley faces and dozens of other such symbols.

More: This opens a menu with options to create bulleted and numbered lists, as well as to redo or undo the most recent editing or formatting.

- **Attachments:** To add file attachments to your e-mail, click or tap the Attachments icon on the left side of the App bar and then select the files using the Start screen's file navigator.

At the upper right of the screen, click the Send button (the flying-envelope icon) to send your message; or, click the Cancel button (the X icon) and then choose Save Draft to save the message for later (such as to finish writing it) or Delete (to remove the message and not send it). You can also save a draft at any time while composing an e-mail by clicking or tapping the Save Draft icon in the App bar — that's safer than using the Cancel button, because it's easy to mistakenly choose Delete Draft from its menu.

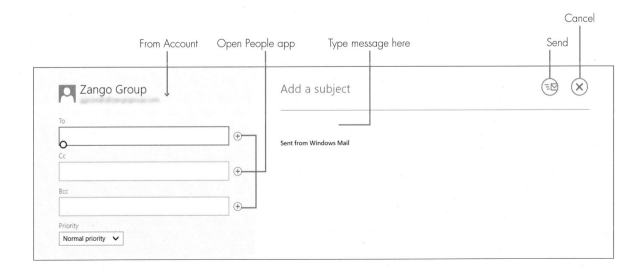

TIP

You can also click or tap the small + icon to the right of the To or Cc field to open the People app (your address book) and select a person from its list. (Use To for the direct recipients of the e-mail and Cc for the indirect recipients, those who need to be kept in the loop.)

The App bar's editing and formatting controls for mail messages

Working with e-mails

The Mail app works very much like other mail apps you've likely used, though its user interface is much cleaner. Here are the main controls to note:

- **Accounts and folders:** Click or tap an account to see its folders and messages. Click a folder to see any messages in it. Note that you can't add, delete, move, or rename folders in Mail. But you can move messages among folders by selecting the message in the message list, opening the App bar, clicking or tapping the Move icon, and then clicking or tapping the desired folder.

- **Message list:** The message list shows the name of the person who sent the e-mail, the day or date received, and the subject line. It may also show a picture of the person if the image is in his or her e-mail or in your address book. If a message is displayed in bold text in the message list, you haven't read it. You may also see a paperclip icon, which indicates that the message has files attached, or you may see a ! icon to indicate a high-priority message or a ↓ icon to indicate a low-priority message.

- **Attachments:** If a message has one or more files attached, a paperclip icon appears to the right of the sender's name in the message list and in the message itself. Click the icon in the message itself to download the files to your PC.

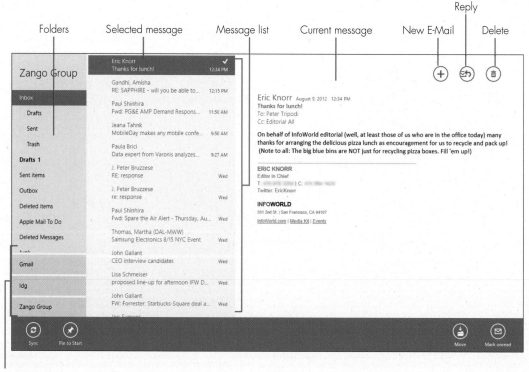

DUMMIES

3

1

Use the Sync icon on the App bar to check for new messages. Mail checks periodically on its own, but you can force an immediate check using this icon. Use the Pin to Start icon to create a tile on the Start screen for the current mailbox — a handy way to see at a glance whether a specific account has new messages.

If you have a physical keyboard and a mouse, you can select multiple messages from the message list: Shift+click a range or Ctrl+click multiple individual messages and then click or tap the Delete icon. On a touchscreen PC with no mouse, you can tap the first desired message; then on a physical keyboard (you can't do this with the onscreen keyboard), hold down Shift and use the ↑ or ↓ keys to select the range from there, releasing Shift when done. Or tap the first message, hold down Ctrl, and move to the next desired message and then press Enter to add it to the selection; repeat this sequence for each desired selection. Unfortunately, there's no way to select multiple messages using only touch gestures.

✔ **Reply, Reply to All, and Forward:** When reading a message, click or tap the Reply icon to open a menu with the Reply, Reply All, and Forward options. Select the desired option for, respectively, replying to just the sender, replying to all recipients, or forwarding the message to others whom you choose. A new message appears containing the original message; enter your additional message, if any, at the top.

✔ **Mark Unread:** If you want to mark a message as unread, such as to remind you to act on it later, select the message in the message list, open the App bar, and click or tap the Mark Unread icon. The message will be bolded in the message list.

As previously noted, Mail is a basic app, lacking many capabilities found in other mail applications. For example, you can't set mail rules or junk filtering, set out-of-office messages, set mail signatures, or adjust mail folders, as you can in most mail applications that run in the Windows Desktop.

Accessing E-Mail in Other Apps

Because the Start screen's Mail app is limited in its capabilities, chances are good that you won't use it as your only e-mail app in Windows 8. Many people are likely to use Microsoft Outlook on the Windows Desktop to get the full e-mail experience — after all, it's the corporate standard and comes with most editions of Microsoft Office,

which most people have on their PCs. You can also access your e-mail from websites such as Outlook.com (formerly Hotmail), Yahoo.com, or the website provided by your Internet service provider, most of whom include e-mail accounts in their services. Or you may choose to use another e-mail program, such as Mozilla's free Thunderbird, on the Windows Desktop.

Many people pick one e-mail app and then use websites for access when not at their computer, though plenty of people use the websites only to access their e-mail — there's no right or wrong answer to how to access e-mail.

Because there are so many ways to access e-mail from the Windows Desktop, this text can't cover them all; refer to the documentation for your e-mail app or website. But because many new Windows 8 PCs — but not those that run the Windows RT version of Windows 8 — come with Outlook 2013, here's a quick guide to using it. If you've used Outlook 2010 or earlier, Outlook 2013 will be familiar. The main differences about it are its support for full-screen mode and some of its visual appearance, because it uses some of the spare Start screen interface style even though it is not a Start screen app.

Outlook 2013 displays much more information and many more controls than Mail, though it has all the usual features, such as the ability to move among folders, delete messages, reply to and forward them, and of course create them. In the full-screen view, Outlook 2013 provides the following capabilities that Mail does not:

✔ **Show/hide the accounts and folders:** Hiding the accounts and folders leaves more room for the messages themselves.

✔ **Message sort:** You can sort your messages by date, subject, sender, and other options, as well as show just unread messages.

✔ **Message search:** You can search your messages in all or selected mailboxes for specific text, to help find specific messages.

✔ **Conversations view:** You can see all related messages to the current one, and even filter those messages by the person who sent them.

✔ **Reply indicators:** You can see at a glance which messages you've replied to.

✔ **Switch to related capabilities:** Using the Mail, Calendar, People, and Tasks links at the bottom of the screen, you can switch to these views for your Exchange, Google, or other account that supports all or some of these features in addition to just e-mail, without having to open different applications.

If you exit full-screen mode to open the Ribbon, you get the dozens of other capabilities that Outlook 2013 offers, such as managing mail rules, junk filters, out-of-office notifications, meeting invitations, and message views, as well as integrating with other Microsoft services such as Lync online conferencing.

But Outlook 2013 has some drawbacks. One is that on a smaller display, such as a PC tablet, its text and buttons are often too small to read and accurately tap (so you may want to carry a stylus and a pair of reading glasses with you). The other is that some features are hidden, such as the feature to close an open e-mail and return to the message list. (Click or tap File to open a bar on the left side of the screen and then click or tap its Close option.) That File bar also is where you set up new accounts, import and export messages, and open the Outlook Options dialog box for advanced settings.

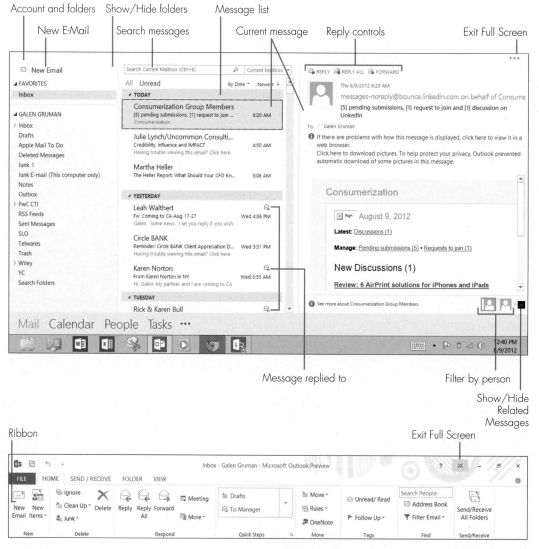

Outlook 2013 in full-screen mode (top) and regular mode (bottom)

FOR DUMMIES

Going Social

O ne of the cool-est capabilities in Windows 8 is its People app, which integrates many social networking services and your contacts and personal profile into one place, giving you a hub for much of your social activities. Sure you can still go to your favorite social networks' websites or use dedicated apps for them in the Start screen or Windows Desktop environments, but you'll likely spend much of your social time using the Start screen's People app instead.

People integrates information and activities across people in your Microsoft, Hotmail/Outlook.com, Outlook/Exchange, Google (Gmail), LinkedIn, Facebook, and Twitter accounts — if you link them to the People app, that is. You can link any or all, getting access to all the user profiles stored in them for use not only in the People app but also in e-mails and instant messaging.

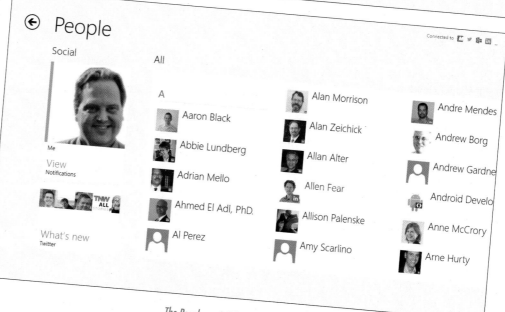

The People app's What's New social network view (top) and People contacts view (bottom)

The People app has three basic components, each with its own pane:

- **People:** This is your address book, storing contact information and related information such as websites and access to social networking streams for each person in the accounts you connect to.

- **What's New:** This is a consolidated view of all the tweets, posts, and updates from your contacts' social media activities.

- **Me:** This is your profile, where you choose how much information to share with others and connect your own feeds so you can see all of your activity in one place as well.

You can have more than one of the same type of account linked to the People app, such as several Twitter accounts, if you want, in addition to having multiple types of accounts linked to it. To link accounts to the People app, open the app and follow these steps:

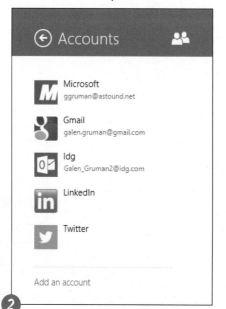

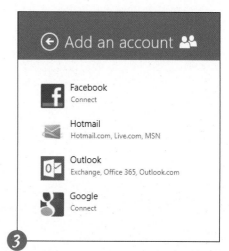

1 Open the Settings charm and click or tap the Accounts link.

2 Any existing accounts display at top. Click or tap the Add an Account link to add an additional account.

3 Click or tap the desired account type from the list; then follow the instructions on the screen that appears, which differ significantly for each type of account.

You can change an account's settings at any time from the Settings charm. Repeat Steps 1 and 2, except in Step 2 click or tap an existing account. Then update its settings in the fields that appear, and click or tap elsewhere when done.

DUMMIES

Social Networking with the People App

After you link accounts to the People app, any that include feeds update the What's New pane of the People app whenever your PC is connected to the Internet. You see a tile for each update, with the most recent on the left. Scroll through the tiles to peruse the updates. To get to the What's New pane, click or tap the What's New link in the Social section on the main People screen.

In the tiles, you'll see any relevant controls for that social service, such as Retweet for Twitter accounts, so you can engage with the item directly from its tile. If you click or tap a tile, you see more context for the person, based on what he or she has chosen to share. Click or tap a person's picture to get a profile screen from which you can click or tap View All to see all of his or her recent posts.

 To go back to the What's New tiles or the main People screen, click or tap the Back button (the ← icon) at the upper left of the screen.

To initiate social networking posts from the People app, open your Me pane by clicking or tapping your photo in the Social section of the main People screen. You see your social accounts listed. Enter your post in the appropriate text field and press Enter to send it.

You can also initiate posts using these methods:

- In a content-oriented application such as Internet Explorer, open the Share charm and then click or tap People from the list of options, if it's available. Then choose your desired service from the menu that appears to open a pane in which you enter your post and send it.

- Click the social service's icon in any tile in People's What's New pane to launch the service's website in Internet Explorer 10 and make your updates from there.

- For social services that have Windows Desktop or Start screen apps, you can install them and switch to them via the Start screen.

TIP To force the PC to update the What's New tiles when in the What's New pane, click or tap the Refresh icon in the App bar.

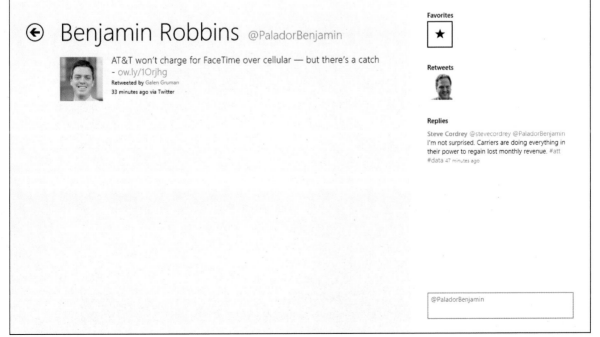

The detailed view of a person's social networking post

Working with Contacts

You can't communicate without contacts, and the People app is your main way to manage your contacts in Windows 8. Not only do the Start screen's Mail, Messages, and People apps use it to find addressee's contact information, but so do any applications (such as Outlook) on the Windows Desktop that use the venerable Windows Address Book. In Windows 8, the Windows Address Book and People use the same contact information and keep it all updated across the two environments. (For all practical purposes, the Address Book is no longer an app on the Windows Desktop. It's now just a service stored in the Program Files (x86) folder so older Windows applications can still access it.)

A person's contact card

In the People app, you can view the details of a person's contact information by clicking or tapping his or her tile. What displays is based on what information you have for that person in the account it came from — it could be a local card entered in your PC, a card based on information stored in an account such as your Microsoft account or Google contacts, or a card based on a person's profile in a social networking service such as Facebook or Twitter. If people have social network feeds, you can see their recent posts listed in their contact cards, as well as the View All link, which you can click or tap to see all their recent activity.

If the information in a card is actionable, clicking or tapping it performs that action. For example, clicking or tapping Send Email opens a menu where you choose where to send a new e-mail from. (If a person has multiple accounts, choose the desired e-mail address from the ⌄ menu to

the right.) Clicking or tapping Map Address opens IE 10 into Bing Maps and displays a map of the address, city, or whatever geographic information is available. And clicking or tapping View Profile opens the social network profile displayed. (Again, use the ⌄ menu to change the profile for people who have several social network profiles.)

But you're not limited to the information from those sources; you can add information to any contact no matter where the initial information came from. To edit the contact information for that contact card, click or tap the Edit icon on the App bar and then add the information you have.

If a person has multiple profiles (from multiple services), click or tap the Link icon on the App bar to see them all and connect them to other profiles not listed by clicking or tapping Choose a Contact. Click or tap the Save icon when done, or click or tap Cancel to not save your new links.

Adding a new contact

FOR DUMMIES

To jump to a person's contact card, rather than scroll through the People app, just type the first letter of the person's first name on a physical keyboard. (Unfortunately, you can't use the onscreen keyboard on a tablet PC to do so.)

The beauty of tying a contact to an account is that the contact is synced to all computers and devices that are signed into that account, so you have to enter it only once, and whenever you update it, it's automatically synced to all other devices using that account.

To add a new contact, go to the People pane and click or tap the New icon on the App bar. An empty contact card displays, ready for you to fill in the information you have. It's the same card you would see when editing an existing contact, except no information is filled in.

There's one other important difference when creating a new card: the Account menu. Use it to specify where that contact information is stored, based on the online accounts you have available, such as your Microsoft account, Exchange account, or Google Gmail account. After you're done entering the information, click or tap the Save icon in the App bar.

By default, People shows contacts in alphabetical order by first name (or company name). To sort by last name instead, open the People app's Settings pane and go to the Options pane. Set the Sort My Contacts by Last Name switch to On. You can also hide contacts from specific accounts in that pane by deselecting them in the list of active accounts.

Working with Your Profile

The final pane in the People app is Me, which shows your profile, including any recent social networking posts. (To open it, click your picture in the Social section of the main People screen.) It works very much like anyone's contact card, letting you see all recent updates you made and any notifications (posts) others have made. But it has two other special options:

- **Click or tap View Profile to view and/or modify your social networking profile in that service's website.** The service is listed below the View Profile link, and you can use the ∨ menu to select a different service if you have multiple social networking services.

- **On the App bar, click or tap the Edit icon to open Microsoft's Windows Live service in Internet Explorer.** Here, you edit your Microsoft account profile, including your contact information, photo, bio, connected social networking accounts, and how much of the personal information is made public (via the Privacy Settings link in the Profile pane, which you switch to by using the options on the left side of the web page).

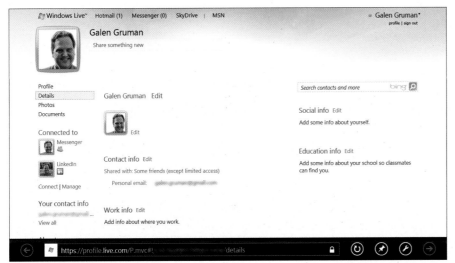

A master profile in Windows Live

Chatting through Messaging

A computing staple for decades, instant messaging apps let you exchange messages with other online friends. Unlike e-mail, instant messaging takes place, well, *instantly:* The screen displays two panes: The right pane displays the messages comprising the conversation, and is where you type in your part of the chat. The left pane shows all conversations (called *threads*); you can switch among them by clicking or tapping the desired thread.

The Messaging app in the Start screen is where you do your instant messaging in Windows 8. Even if your online friends use different messaging services and programs, the Messaging app can swap messages with them all.

To chat with someone, he has to be added as a friend to your Windows Live account. To add people as friends to Windows Live, open the App bar and click or tap the Invite icon. This action opens the Windows Live website, where you can add people who use any of the following accounts: AOL Mail, Facebook, Gmail, Hi5, Hyves, LinkedIn, Outlook, Tagged, or Windows Messenger. They're sent an invite via e-mail and must respond to become friends.

After a person confirms you as a friend, his instant-messaging information is added to the People app — you can't add it in the contact card yourself. At that point, you can initiate an instant-messaging session by clicking or tapping the New icon on the App bar, and then choosing the person's name from the People pane that appears.

In the Messaging app, enter your text in the text field at the bottom of the right pane and press Enter to send that text to the other person. You'll see his reply in the main window, with your messages alternating in the order sent.

You can have multiple conversations, and the conversations are divided into threads. The Threads section is at the left of the Messaging app, and to switch among threads all you need to do is click or tap the person's name whose conversation you want to switch to.

It's all very simple to do after you set up your friends.

TIP

To delete a conversation, open the App bar and then click or tap the Delete icon. And if you don't want to be bothered with conversations for a while, click or tap the App bar's Status icon and choose Invisible from the menu that appears. That keeps you from showing up as available in your friends' messaging programs. To reappear to your circle of friends, click or tap the Status icon and choose Online.

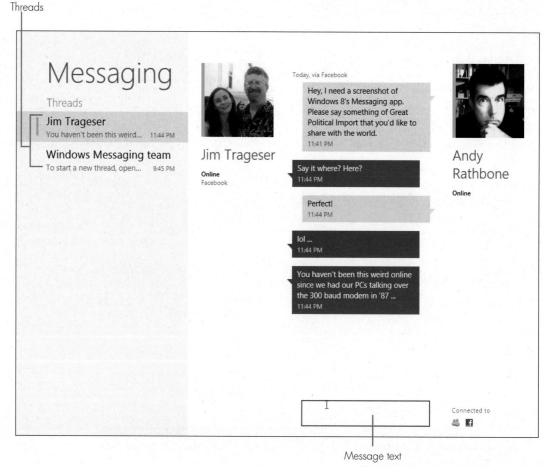

Threads

Message text

An instant-messaging conversation in the Messaging app

DUMMIES

Managing Your Life

The Windows 8 Start screen environment gives you a nice selection of apps to keep up on the news and other information that matters to you in a visually striking presentation. You can keep up on news, weather, sports, and finances by using content provided by Microsoft's Bing search engine in apps for each content type. There are also Start screen apps for travel and maps to help you explore the world — or at least navigate it! And you can keep your calendar under control using the Calendar app.

Not all of the handy apps in Windows 8 are provided in the Start screen environment; the Windows Desktop also has some handy apps for everyday use, such as its Notepad and WordPad editing tools. But whether you're using the Start screen or Windows Desktop environment, you'll find Windows 8 makes it easy to stay informed and keep your life organized.

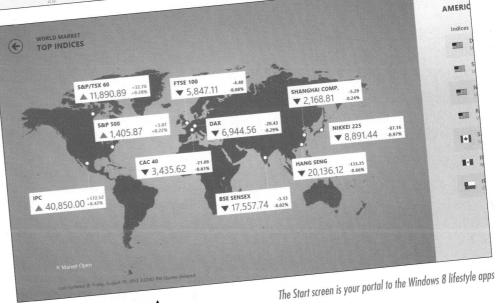

The Start screen is your portal to the Windows 8 lifestyle apps

TIP

You can get more Start screen apps from the Windows Store (through the Store app) — both free and paid — to add capabilities and entertainment options to your PC. And you can install traditional Windows Desktop apps that you download from online stores or buy from a retailer and install from a CD or DVD.

Staying Up-to-Date

The four Bing-based information apps are handy for staying informed: News, Weather, Finance, and Sports. All four are Start screen apps and work similarly. The top story displays on the first screen (in the case of the Weather app, the current location's weather displays), and you can scroll through panes for additional stories (or, for Weather, more details such as historic data).

The News and Sports apps have no App bars, whereas the Finances and Weather apps do, though with minimal controls. All four apps provide additional content options on the Control bar (the bar you can display at the top of some apps by right-clicking or, on a touchscreen, swiping up from the bottom edge or down from the top edge).

The News app's options:

- **Bing Daily** shows the top news stories gathered by Microsoft. Scroll to see various sections such as Business and World. Click or tap a section label to see just stories in the section and click or tap a story to read it in full.

- **My News** lets you create your own news sections based on keywords you enter; these sections appear only in this pane.

- **Sources** lists all the places that Microsoft draws its news from; click or tap a source's tile to see stories just from that source.

The Sports app's options:

- **Today** shows the top sport stories of the day.

- **Favorite Teams** lets you track news and stats on the teams whose names you enter there. After you add your teams, click or tap a tile to see news and stats for that team.

- **The other panes** provide news for the specific sports and leagues named in the tiles. The only App bar control is to refresh the information, such as for scores.

The Finances app's options:

- **Today** gives the latest market figures and top news stories.

- **Watchlist** lets you add stocks and funds to track their performance; in the App bar, you can pin the watchlist to the Start screen.

- **News** shows the top financial and economic news stories.

- **Rates** shows a selection of rates for mortgages, savings, and common loan types. Click or tap a label to open a page with a list of providers' specific rates, based on your current location.

- **Currencies** displays current currency values for dozens of countries. Click or tap the Converter icon (on the first screen and on the App bar) to have the app convert an amount of your choice between the currencies of your choosing.

- **World Market** shows at a glance the current performance of major stock market indexes.

- **Best of Web** shows Microsoft's recommended websites for personal finance information and resources.

The Weather app's options:

- **Home** shows the weather in the current location. Scroll to get more details on the weather, such as the hourly forecast and historical trends.

- **Places** lets you add specific cities to its page, so you can easily check the weather in those cities. Click or tap a tile to get detailed weather information for that city.

- **World Weather** shows you at a glance the weather in major cities. Click or tap a country or region on the map to zoom in and get details for more cities in that area.

TIP

In the Weather app's Settings charm, you set whether temperatures are displayed in Fahrenheit or Celsius, and you can temporarily switch to the other system at any time via the App bar's Change To icon.

Organizing Your Calendar

Keeping track of your appointments, birthdays, and so on can be difficult to do in your head, and that's why people use calendars to track events. PCs of course long ago raised calendars to a new level, with events that are easily moved, can issue reminders, and can be set to repeat automatically. If you use server-based tools such as Exchange or Google Calendar, you can even monitor and work with your calendar from multiple devices.

Windows 8 has its own Calendar app, a Start screen application that syncs to Exchange, Google Calendar, and Hotmail/Outlook.com, so your calendar is available and updated across multiple devices. It has all the capabilities you'd expect from a calendar app: support for multiple calendars (each is color-coded), repeating events, reminders, and invitations.

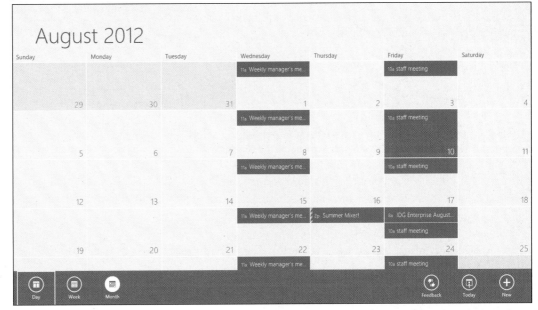

The Calendar app

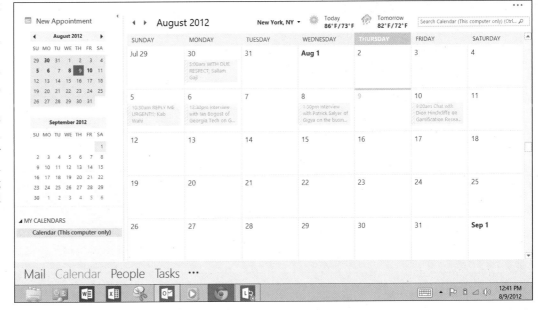

The optional Outlook application

The Calendar app is easy to use. When you open it the first time, you get the month view; just scroll to see the preceding and following months. Use the App bar's Day, Week, and Month icons to switch views to one that you prefer at the moment. For example, the month view is great to get an overview of your schedule, whereas the Day view lets you see all the activities you need to do today in detail.

There are several activities that Calendar doesn't support that you may use at work with Microsoft Outlook (usually included with Microsoft Office) and an Exchange server. For example, Outlook can display the local weather, search your calendar, change the current time zone, create complex recurring event patterns, and manage other calendars delegated to you. If you have such needs, you should use Outlook. But note that because Outlook and Calendar both sync to Exchange, you can use both calendar apps in Windows 8, using Calendar for basic needs and switching to Outlook for the more complex options.

TIP

Click or tap the Today icon in the App view to quickly jump to today's calendar. It's a handy way to get back to your current schedule after, say, entering the no-classes dates for next year's school calendar.

To add an event, click or tap in your calendar at the desired date and time (the Day view works best for this). In the screen that opens, enter the relevant details in the Details pane at left. And in the pane at right, click or tap Add a Title and type in a title for your event; then click or tap the blank area between the horizontal line to type in any other details or notes you want saved with the event. Here are the options for the Details pane; note some will vary based on the calendar's capabilities:

- **Where:** Type in a location for the event, such as an address or a conference room. (This field is optional.)

- **When:** Click or tap the menus for the month, day, and year to change them. By default, the date you clicked or tapped on your calendar when creating the event is displayed.

- **Start:** Use the menus for the hour, minute, and AM/PM settings to set the start time for the event.

- **How Long:** Use the menu to select how long the event will run; choose Custom to specify the end date and time. (The End option appears to set this information.)

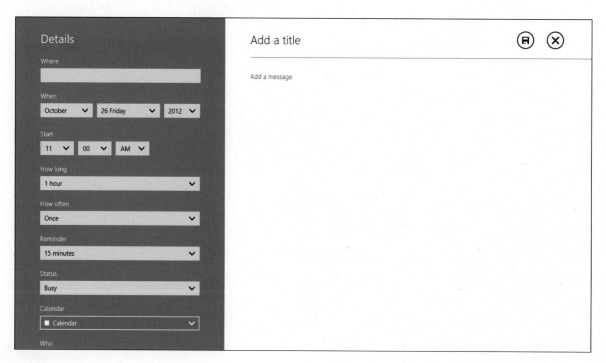

The Details pane when adding an event

DUMMIES

✔ **How Often:** Use the menu to make this event a repeating event, if you want. Your choices are Once, Every Day, Every Weekday, Every Week, Every Week, Every Month, and Every Year. If you want more complex repeating events, such as every third Wednesday, you need to use another app, such as Outlook, instead of Calendar.

✔ **Reminder:** Use the menu to set when you receive a reminder alert about the appointment (so you don't forget it or get there late!).

✔ **Status:** Use this menu to indicate in Outlook or other compatible shared calendars your availability, so people know whether they can schedule you for a meeting on their calendar. The options are Free, Busy, Tentative, Out of Office, and Working Elsewhere.

✔ **Calendar:** If you set up multiple calendar accounts, use this to specify which calendar it is assigned to. Doing so tells Windows 8 which calendar to sync the event to. (You might have one for work using Exchange and one for home using Google Calendar, for example.) Each calendar has its own color, so you can see at a glance which calendar an event is on. To set up accounts, open the Settings charm, click or tap Accounts, click or tap Add an Account, and choose the desired calendar service.

✔ **Who:** If you want to send invitations to other people to join the event (if your calendar account supports this feature), enter their e-mail addresses in this field, separated by commas.

Shockingly, Windows 8 doesn't look up names you enter in the People app to find their e-mail addresses for you. The people you invite get an invitation via e-mail with an invitation file attached (it has the file extension .ics), which many apps use to add the event to their calendars automatically. In the Calendar app, any invitations you receive are automatically added to your calendar and indicated with a dashed line on the left side. Click or tap such an invitation event to open it and click or tap the Respond icon on the App bar to accept or decline the invitation.

When you click or tap an event, it opens to show its Details pane, where you can modify the event or simply review its details. If the event is a repeating event, you'll get a menu with two options that you must select from before you can edit the event:

✔ **Change One** changes just that specific instance.

✔ **Change All** affects all occurrences.

For any event you've opened, click the Save icon button (a disk icon) to save any changes and the Cancel icon button (an X icon) to close the event, both at the upper right of the screen. To delete an event, open it and then click or tap Delete from the App bar.

In addition to letting you set up calendars, the Settings charm for the Calendar app provides other options you can adjust for those calendars. In the Settings charm, click or tap Options to open a pane with these options. You'll see a section for each calendar account, with the Show switch to control whether that account displays in Calendar and menus to change the color of that account's events. The calendar associated with your Microsoft account also lets you select the color for birthdays and U.S. holidays in the calendar.

The Options pane for Calendar's Settings charm

Reading and Writing Documents

Most people use PCs to work on documents, at least at some point, including party invitations, homework, reports for the office, and more. You probably also receive reports and other documents to read and sometimes edit.

Documents tend to come in four common formats, though there are others in use:

- **Adobe Portable Document Format (PDF):** A read-only format that presents pages intact with all layout and formatting. You can read such documents in the Start screen's Windows Reader app.

- **Microsoft Word (.doc and .docx):** The document format most of the world uses, created by Microsoft and the standard for its Word application but supported by many other programs. The WordPad app that comes with the Windows Desktop environment can create and edit Word files, though it doesn't support all of its capabilities.

- **Rich Text Format (RTF):** A document format widely supported, it's similar to the Word format in its capabilities for formatting. The WordPad app also can create and edit RTF files.

- **Text-only files (.txt):** The original document format supports just text — no formatting — and is essentially the lowest-common-denominator format for text. WordPad and the included Notepad app on the Windows Desktop can create and edit such files.

When you double-click or double-tap a file in File Explorer or open a file from a website or in an e-mail, Windows opens the file with the application it's set to use as the default. For PDFs, that default is Windows Reader; for Word and RTF documents, it's WordPad or, if it's installed, Microsoft Word; and for text-only files, it's Notepad unless Word is installed.

Using Reader

The Reader app is what it claims to be: a reader, for PDF files. On the App bar, you have just a few options, most related to viewing the PDF file:

- **Find** searches the PDF for the text you specify.

- **Cover Page,** if selected, tells Reader that the first page of the PDF file is a cover image and should be viewed as its own page when you are in side-by-side view. (Thus, the icon appears only if you're viewing the PDF in side-by-side view.)

- **Two Pages, One Page,** and **Continuous** control the appearance of the PDF file onscreen. Two Pages shows pages side by side, whereas One Page shows just one page per screen. Continuous removes the space between pages, as if the document were a long scroll.

- **Open** and **Save As** do what you'd expect: Respectively, they open a file from the PC and save the current file to the PC. You navigate to the desired hard disk and folder by using the Start screen's file navigator. The Save icon appears if you've added highlighting or notes to the PDF.

- **More** opens a menu with four options. **Rotate** pivots the page in 90-degree angles because some PDFs are rotated when created, and it's too hard to turn your head 90 degrees to read them. **Info** shows information about the PDF, such as the creation date and number of pages. **Bookmarks** lets you jump to pages bookmarked by the PDF's creator; a list of available bookmarks appears in a menu. And **Close File** closes the PDF, removing it from view.

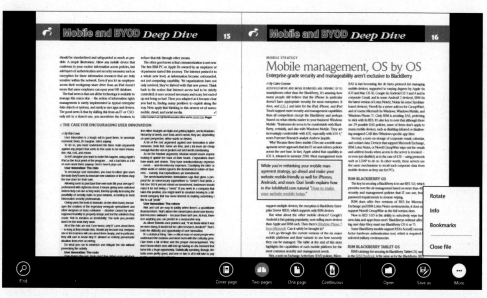

The Reader app for viewing PDF files

DUMMIES

Here's how to perform basic tasks with Reader:

- ✔ **Navigate:** You typically move through the PDF by scrolling its pages. But if the PDF has bookmarks, they help you move to a desired section faster.

- ✔ **Annotate:** You can do basic annotations in Windows Reader as well. For example, select text you want to highlight, and right-click the selection to open a menu from which you choose Highlight. (On a touchscreen, the menu appears if you tap one of the selection handles.) Selecting the text the same way again gives you the Remove Highlight option.

- ✔ **Add notes:** You can add a note instead by choosing Add a Note, typing in the note's text, and clicking or tapping elsewhere in the PDF. This places a note icon near the text. Right-click or tap that note icon to open a menu with the Open Note and Delete Note options.

- ✔ **Copy text:** You can copy selected text by choosing the Copy option.

Using WordPad

If you really want and need formatting but you lack Microsoft Word or some other word processing software, Windows WordPad will do.

Although WordPad is a Windows Desktop application, if you have a physical keyboard, you can open it from the Start screen by typing **wordpad** and choosing WordPad from the results. It's also available as a tile in the Start screen if you open the App bar and click All Apps. If you use it a lot, you may want to pin it to the Start screen and the Windows Desktop taskbar.

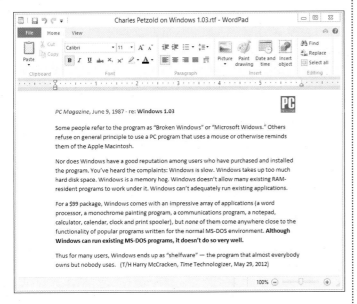

WordPad

If you're just starting out with WordPad, keep these facts in mind:

- ✔ **To format text,** select the text you want to format and then choose the formatting you want from the Font group on the Ribbon's Home tab. For example, to change the font, click or tap the ⌄ menu next to the font name and choose the font you like.

- ✔ **To format a paragraph,** simply click once inside the paragraph and choose the formatting you want from the Ribbon's Paragraph group.

- ✔ **General page layout is controlled by settings in the Page Setup dialog box.** General page layout includes things such as margins and whether the page is printed vertically or horizontally. To open the dialog box, choose File➪Page Setup.

- ✔ **Tabs are complicated.** Every paragraph starts with tab stops set every half inch. You set additional tab stops by clicking in the middle of the ruler. (You can also set them by clicking the tiny side arrow to the right of the word *Paragraph* and then clicking or tapping the Tabs button.) The tab stops that you set up work only in individual paragraphs: Select one paragraph and set a tab stop, and it works only in the selected paragraph; select three paragraphs and set the stop, and it works in all three.

- ✔ **You can save in several formats,** including Word's .docx (but not .doc), RTF, OpenOffice (.odt, used by the free LibreOffice and OpenOffice apps), and text-only (.txt; note that all formatting and embedded images are removed).

WordPad has a few worthwhile features: bullets and numbered lists; paragraph justification; line spacing; super- and subscript; and indent. However, WordPad lacks many of the features that you may have come to expect from other word processors. For example, you can't even insert a page break, much less a table. If you spend time writing anything but the most straightforward documents, you'll outgrow WordPad quickly. But if your documents are plain, WordPad is a simple and free alternative to the much more complex Word.

Using Notepad

Reaching back into the primordial days of personal computing, Notepad was conceived, designed, and developed by programmers, for programmers — and it shows. Although Notepad has been vastly improved over the years, many of the old limitations persist. Still, if you want a fast, no-nonsense text editor (certainly nobody would have the temerity to call Notepad a word processor), Notepad's a decent choice.

Notepad understands only plain, simple, unformatted text — basically the stuff you see on your keyboard. It doesn't support formatting such as bold text, embedded pictures, and hyperlinks to web pages.

If you have a physical keyboard, you can open Notepad from the Start screen by typing **notepad** and choosing Notepad from the search results. It's also available as a tile on the Start screen if you open the App bar and click All Apps. If you use it a lot, save some time by pinning it to the Start screen and the Windows Desktop taskbar.

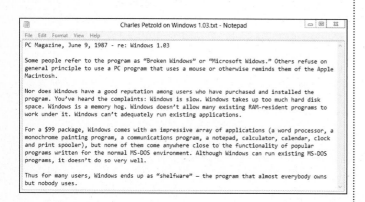

Notepad

When using Notepad, you'll find the following tidbits of advice very helpful:

- **Notepad can handle files up to about 48MB in size.** (That's not quite the size of the *Encyclopedia Britannica,* but it's close.) If you try to open a file that's larger, an alert box suggests that you open the file with a different editor.

- **You can change the font, sorta.** When you first start Notepad, it displays a file's contents in the 10-point Lucida Console font. That font was chosen by Notepad's designers because it's relatively easy to see on most computer monitors. To change the font that's displayed onscreen, choose Format➜Font and pick one from the submenu. Just remember that the font is used only for your visual pleasure while working in Notepad — the font isn't actually applied to the text or saved in the document.

- **You can wrap text, too.** Usually text extends way off the right side of the screen. That's intentional. Notepad, ever true to the file it's attached to, skips to a new line only when it encounters a line break — usually when someone presses Enter, which typically occurs at the end of every paragraph. But if you don't want to scroll all the way to the right to read every paragraph, choose Format➜Word Wrap.

Manipulating text

Almost everyone who uses a PC knows the basics of manipulating text, but it's worth a refresher — especially if you're using a touchscreen PC:

- **To select text with a keyboard:** Move the cursor to the beginning of the text you want to select, hold down the Shift key, and move the cursor to the end of the desired selection. Release the Shift key; the selected text is highlighted.

- **To select text with a mouse:** Move the cursor to the beginning of the text you want to select, hold down the mouse button, and move the cursor to the end of the desired selection. Release the mouse button; the selected text is highlighted.

- **To select text with your finger:** Tap on the first word you want to be in the text selection; the entire word is highlighted, and two selection handles appear, one on either end. Tap and drag a selection handle to a new location; the text between that new location and the originally selected word is now selected; you can use either or both selection handles to change the range.

After you select text, you can copy and paste it, delete it, or move it:

- **To copy and paste text:** Press Ctrl+C, click or tap the Copy button on the app's Ribbon (if it has one), or tap a selection handle and choose Copy. Move the cursor to the destination (it may be another document and/or app), and press Ctrl+V, click or tap the Paste button on the app's Ribbon (if it has one), or tap a selection handle and choose Paste.

- **To delete text:** Press Ctrl+X if you want to be able to paste it later (such as to move it) or press Backspace or Del to delete it without being able to paste it elsewhere.

- **To move text:** Cut and paste it. In some apps, you can simply drag the selection to a new location.

Depending on the app you're using, you may also have formatting options for text selections, such as applying italics or a colored background.

The Consumer Privacy Bill of Rights applies comprehensive, globally recognized Fair Information Practice Principles (FIPPs) to the interactive and highly interconnected environment in which we live and work today. Specifically, it provides for:

- Individual Control: Consumers have a right to exercise control over what personal data companies collect from them and how they use it.

- Transparency: Consumers have a right to easily understandable and accessible information about privacy and security practices.

Selecting text via touch

Mapping and Traveling the World

Windows 8 provides two apps to help you get around. They're both Start screen apps: Maps and Travel. As you'd expect, Maps displays maps and provides directions between any two locations. Travel combines travel guides with flight and hotel booking features to help you explore trip options and even make them happen.

Using the Maps app

The Maps app is simple and will be familiar to you if you've used a maps app on a smartphone. But note it won't work if you don't have a live Internet connection.

Here are the options available on the Maps App bar:

- **My Location:** When you open Maps, it usually displays your current location. If not, you can quickly go there (assuming it can find you — Maps will ask your permission the first time to detect your location) by clicking or tapping the My Location icon on the App bar.

- **Map Style:** You can adjust the view between aerial photography and traditional roadmap by using the Map Style icon on the App bar.

- **Show Traffic:** You can display or hide current traffic conditions by using the App bar's Show Traffic icon. The app will color roads based on their traffic: Green means traffic is flowing at or near the speed limit, yellow means it is slow but moving at an acceptable rate, and red means it's stop-and-go — or simply stopped.

- **Directions:** Click or tap the Directions icon on the App bar to open the Directions pane, where you tell Maps the start and end points of your travel plans. Normally, the start point (A) is your current location, but you can reverse that by clicking the Reverse direction icon to the right of the Start field. After you enter the two locations, press Enter or click the → button to have Maps map out the trip. It displays each stage at the top of the screen, and you scroll through them until you reach your destination.

The Maps app in aerial view

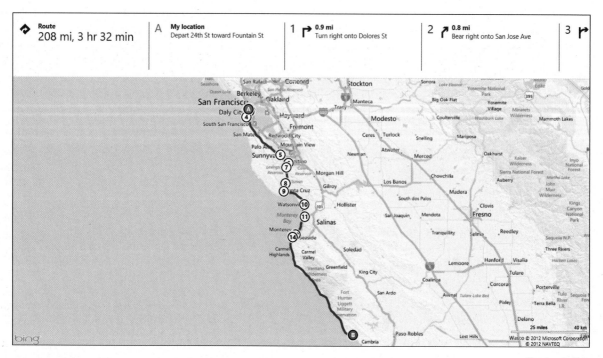

Route 208 mi, 3 hr 32 min	A	My location Depart 24th St toward Fountain St	1	0.9 mi Turn right onto Dolores St	2	0.8 mi Bear right onto San Jose Ave	3

Directions in Maps

The easiest way to see a map of a certain location is to open the Search charm and enter in the destination, whether a city, full address, or landmark. On a touchscreen, you can also use the pinch and expand gestures to zoom in and out and then drag your finger to scroll through the map to explore the world as it moves onscreen. On a non-touch-enabled PC, two large icons appear on the left side of the screen: + to zoom in and – to zoom out. Click and drag the mouse to scroll the screen.

TIP

If you want to get directions from your current location but the Start field doesn't display My Location, go to the App bar, click or tap My Location, and then return to the Directions pane — that usually adds your current location as the starting point.

TIP

If your device has GPS, Maps will monitor your location as you move, so you can follow your progress. Just don't be the driver when using that feature!

DUMMIES

Using the Travel app

The Travel app is also simple, though it offers several capabilities in its five panes:

- **Home:** This displays a variety of travel features, panoramic images, and articles — it's where you get to dream about where you might travel.

- **Destinations:** This displays tiles for dozens of popular vacation destinations. Click or tap one to open a mini travel guide.

- **Flights:** This lets you book flights via Kaya.com as well as check flight status and search schedules. You can also see panoramic photos of various airports if that somehow appeals to you.

- **Hotels:** This lets you make hotel reservations and see panoramic photos of featured hotels.

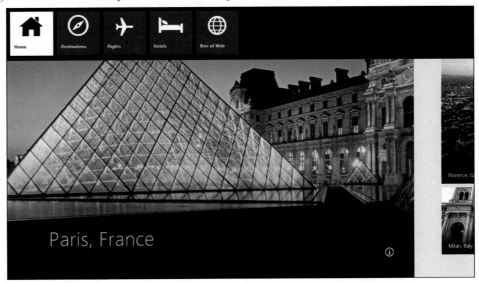

- **Best of Web:** This displays tiles for Microsoft's recommended travel sites; click a tile to go to that website in Internet Explorer.

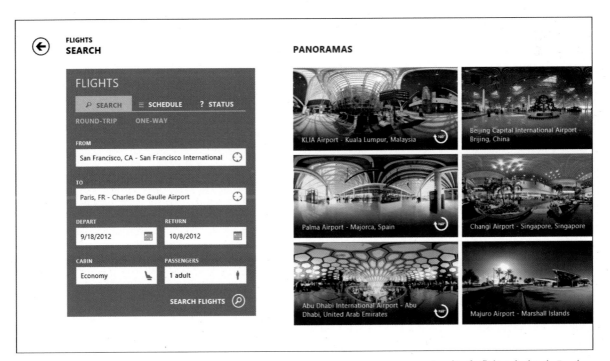

Searching for flights to book in the Travel app

Working with Windows Tools

IN THIS ARTICLE

● *Handy odds and ends* ● *Going under the hood*

Good ol' traditional Windows — what's now called the Windows Desktop — has five handy utilities that remain handy in Windows 8. If you don't already know them, you should. Three are general-purpose apps for all users: Character Map, Calculator, and Sticky Notes. The other two, Task Manager and Command Prompt, are meant for advanced users and IT support staff.

Although these utilities are Windows Desktop apps, you can access them from the Start screen by clicking or tapping All Apps from the App bar or, if you have a physical keyboard, by typing their name and selecting them from the list that appears. You may want to pin these utilities to the Start screen and the Windows Desktop's taskbar if you use them frequently.

Utilities for Everyone

These three utilities are broadly useful, and frankly, it's surprising that there isn't a Start screen version of Calculator nor an ability to create notes-style tiles on the Start screen, and that the capabilities of Character Map aren't available in the Start screen through an onscreen keyboard option.

Character Map

Using the Character Map, you can ferret out characters out of any font, copy them, and then paste them into whatever word processor you may be using (including WordPad).

Windows ships with many *fonts* — collections of characters — and several of those fonts include many interesting characters that you may want to use.

You can use many characters as pictures — arrows, check marks, boxes, and so on — in the various Wingdings and Webding fonts. Copy them into your documents and increase the font size as you like.

Character Map

DUMMIES

Character Map is handy to get characters you probably never knew existed, but you can also get many accented characters and special symbols using the onscreen keyboard on touch-enabled devices. There are two ways:

✔ Open the symbols keyboard for the standard onscreen keyboard by tapping the &123 key. Then tap the → key to get various special symbols such as €, ¶, and •. Tap the ← key to go back to the first symbols list. (When done, tap the &123 key to go back to the standard keyboard.)

✔ In the regular onscreen keyboard, tap and hold the following keys to get a menu of related characters (often accented versions) you can select instead: a, c, d, e, g, h, i, j, n, o, s, t, u, y, ', . (period), , (comma), and ?. In the symbols mode (tap &123), tap and hold the following keys to get their variants: ", .!, #, $, %, (,), –, =, +, *, /, and the numerals 0 through 9. Tapping the ☺ key displays an array of emoticons.

Top: The special symbols available in the onscreen keyboard's symbols mode.
Bottom: Many keys if tapped and held display alternate keys available.

Calculator

Windows includes a capable calculator. Actually, Windows contains four capable calculators, with several options in each one.

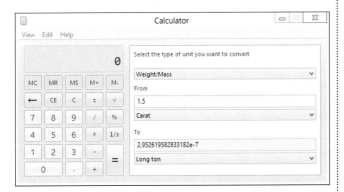

Calculator's Unit Conversion mode

To use the Calculator, type whatever you like on your keyboard or click or tap the keys in the app. Press Enter when you want to carry out the calculation. For example, to calculate 123 times 456, you type, click, or tap **123 * 456** and then press Enter. (Don't use the X key for multiplication — it won't work!)

The Calculator comes in four modes: Standard; Scientific (which adds sin, tan, x to the y, and the like); Programmer (hex, octal, mod, and XOR); and Statistics (averages and summations). You can also choose three options, which appear as a separate slide-out Calculator to the right. Date Calculation makes you choose dates from built-in calendars. The Templates option gives you a quick way to calculate gas mileage, lease payments, and simple mortgage amortization.

Sticky Notes

Do you really like little yellow sticky notes on your screen? Really? Okay, you can get them in the Windows Desktop by using the Sticky Notes app. (At least they won't get your screen gummy!)

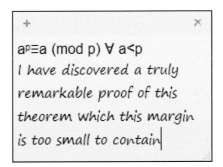

$a^p \equiv a \pmod p \ \forall \ a < p$
I have discovered a truly remarkable proof of this theorem which this margin is too small to contain

Sticky Notes, with copied text to get the special symbols and fonts

Here are a few tips for working with sticky notes:

✔ **Create a new sticky note:** After you write your first sticky note, you can create a new one by clicking or tapping the + icon in the upper-left corner. Delete a note by clicking or tapping the X icon in the upper-right corner.

✔ **Change the color:** You can change the color to something other than that eyestrain-inducing cadmium yellow by right-clicking or tapping and holding on the note and choosing a new color from the contextual menu that appears. Other options include copying and deleting any selected text in the note.

✔ **Move and resize:** Sticky notes live on your desktop. You can drag and move them like any other denizen of the desktop. They're easy to resize — just drag a side or corner.

✔ **Show or hide all sticky notes:** You can alternately show or hide all sticky notes on your desktop by clicking or tapping the Sticky Notes icon on the taskbar — it appears as long as any notes exist.

Utilities for Advanced Users

You can skip the rest of this section if you're not a geek. Well, maybe not skip it — although aimed at advanced users, knowing about these utilities could come in handy one day, even if it's just to know what they can do so you can ask an advanced user for help that you know he or she can deliver.

Task Manager

Sometimes, apps stop responding, or your PC seems to run slowly for no apparent reason. Task Manager helps you deal with these situations. It shows all running apps, and you can select one that isn't responding and click or tap the End Task button. It's a drastic action — all unsaved changes are lost — but sometimes you have no choice.

If you're a more advanced user, click or tap More Details to get the full Task Manager, which shows the Processes pane. The Processes pane displays not just apps that are running but also the pieces of Windows, called *background processes,* that are running behind the scenes. You can see how much memory, processor, and other resources each task takes, so you can quickly identify something that is out of control and hogging your PC's resources, forcing everything else to slow to a crawl. You may need to end that runaway task to get the rest of Windows running smoothly.

The other panes in Task Manager help you understand your PC's operations in more detail and are best left to support staff.

Command Prompt

This one is really for the supergeeky and the IT crowd: Command Prompt opens a dialog box in which you enter textual commands to perform actions on your PC. You've probably heard of DOS, the PC's original way of handling commands. You had to know all those commands and enter them exactly right. Well, Command Prompt basically provides a way to do that in Windows, bypassing all its graphical glory. But it can be useful when trying to repair a PC or do some tasks that can be time-consuming in the regular graphical Windows. Just be sure that whoever uses Command Prompt knows what he or she is doing.

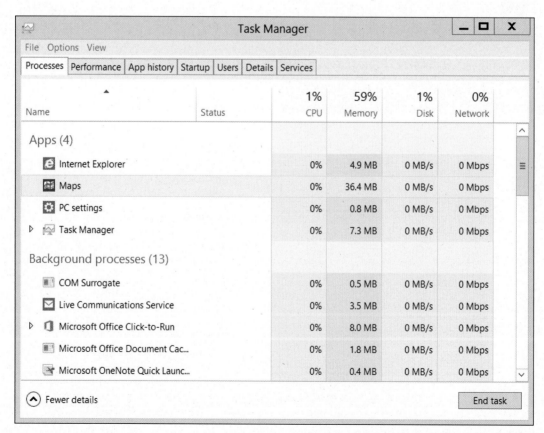

Task Manager's More Details mode, showing the Processes pane

DUMMIES

Taking Pictures

● *Taking photos* ● *Setting camera options* ● *Cropping photos*

T oday's digital cameras are little computers in their own right, so it's natural that Windows 8 treats them like newfound friends. Plug a camera into your PC via a USB cable, turn on the camera, and Windows greets the newcomer, offering to copy your camera's photos onto your computer.

The Photos app

Or just use the camera built into your PC, if it has one — most tablet PCs and many laptops do. In many cases, the quality of the built-in camera is good enough. But if you want more professional-looking pictures, you should use a higher-end digital camera to take those priceless memories.

TIP

After you've begun creating a digital family album on your computer, please back it up properly by turning on File History, the automatic backup feature in Windows 8. Computers will come and go, but your family memories can't be replaced.

Taking Photos with Your PC

If your PC has a built-in camera or you've connected a camera to it via the USB port, you take pictures with the Camera app that lives in the Start screen. The first time you use the Camera app, the screen displays "Can Camera use your webcam and microphone?" Click or tap Allow to continue. (If you don't want to continue, don't click or tap Block unless you never expect to use this app. Instead, simply go back to the Start screen.)

Then follow these steps to take a photo:

1 When the Camera app opens, it shows whatever the camera sees. If you have a PC tablet with front and back cameras, open the App bar and tap the Change Camera icon to switch between the two.

2 (Optional) To give yourself a three-second delay, open the App bar and click or tap the Timer icon. The icon's background becomes white so you know it's enabled.

3 Point the camera at whatever you want to shoot. Note there are no controls, such as Zoom In or Zoom Out. Click or tap the screen to take the photo. If you enabled the timer, you see a three-second countdown onscreen before the image is taken. When the image is taken, you see it quickly head off past the left edge of the screen into your camera roll (and in the Pictures library on your PC), and you can take another photo.

4 To see your photos, you can scroll to the left by using the mouse's wheel or ball. (Scrolling up goes left and scrolling down goes right.) Use the pinch gesture on a touchscreen to see multiple images at once. Scroll back to the rightmost image to see a live image of what the camera sees.

REMEMBER

Your *camera roll* is the set of pictures taken on your PC, which the Camera app lets you review, similar to how a digital camera lets you view the pictures taken on it.

TIP

If you want to take a video instead of a still photo, click or tap the Video Mode icon on the App bar. As long as the icon's background is white, the camera is in Video mode. Click or tap the screen to begin recording. You see a timer onscreen showing the length of the video recording. Click or tap the screen again to end the video capture. Be sure to click or tap the Video Mode icon to switch back to still-photo mode.

TIP

You can take a *screenshot* — a picture of the current screen — by pressing ⊞+PrtScr on a physical keyboard. (A touchscreen or mouse equivalent is not available.) The screen dims slightly to indicate the capture, which is stored automatically in the Screenshots folder in your Pictures library. Use this technique to create your own documentation of problems or something you want to see again later.

Adjusting Camera Settings

You can adjust the camera settings by using the Camera Options icon on the App bar. It opens a pane with the following options:

- **Photo Resolution:** Generally, you want the highest resolution possible to get the best image quality, though that also increases file size. The ratio in parentheses affects how completely the photo will fill a screen or a print. Odds are good that your screen is 16:9, so this ratio may be best for you. Most prints are still 4:3, so you may want that ratio if you know you're going to print the photo. Experiment — you'll see the effect onscreen immediately.

- **Audio Device:** Relevant to video rather than photos, this option is limited to your built-in microphone unless you have more than one mic attached.

- **Video Stabilization:** Stability is good, especially for handheld video, so turn it on to eliminate jitter when you shoot.

- **More:** Choose More to see sliders for Brightness and Contrast, as well as perhaps for Flicker, Focus, and Exposure (depending on your camera's capabilities). Adjust the brightness and contrast settings for the best exposure. Flicker applies to video and generally should be 60 Hz or higher. If you want to focus the lens yourself, set the Focus switch to Manual and then use the slider to determine the focal depth. Likewise, to set the exposure length, set the Exposure switch to Manual and use the slider to change its duration. You'll see onscreen the results of changing the brightness, contrast, and focus settings.

 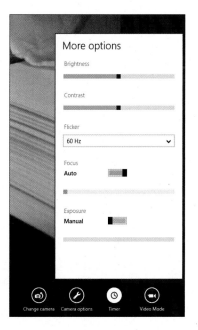

Editing Photos in the Camera Roll

When you're in the Camera app's camera roll, you can crop and delete the photos you've taken. (Scroll to the left on a touchscreen, or up using a mouse's wheel or ball to see the camera roll.) Navigate to the desired photo and then open the App bar.

- **To crop a photo:** Click or tap the Crop icon on the App bar and then use the cropping han-

dles that display onscreen to crop the image as desired. On the App bar, click or tap OK to accept the crop or Cancel to return the photo to its original state.

- **To delete a photo:** Click or tap the Delete icon on the App bar.

Managing Photos

● *Importing photos from a camera* ● *Viewing photos* ● *Editing photos in the Paint app*

1 t's great to be able to take photos from your computer, but chances are good that you have photos you've taken using other cameras or gotten from friends and family that you want to bring into your PC to keep virtual photo albums available for viewing at any time.

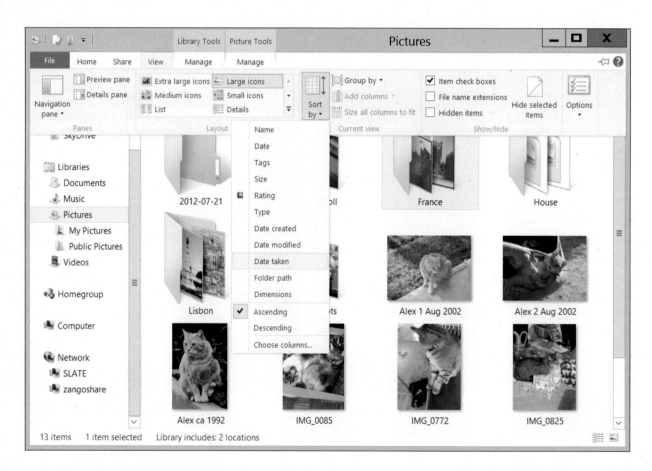

Bringing in Photos from a Camera

Most digital cameras come with software that grabs your camera's photos and places them into your computer when connected via a USB cable. But you often needn't install that software or even bother trying to figure out its menus, thank goodness. That's because Windows 8 easily fetches photos from nearly any make and model of digital camera.

To import your camera's photos into your computer, be sure the picture-taking mode is turned off and the camera is instead set to display or view mode. (If you can see your camera's photos in the viewfinder or viewscreen, you're ready to import them into your PC.) Then follow these steps:

Canon EOS DIGITAL REBEL...

Choose what to do with this device.

Import photos and videos
Photos

Open device to view files
File Explorer

Take no action

1 Connect the camera to your PC by using the cable supplied with the camera. Typically, there's a standard USB plug that goes into your PC and a smaller plug that goes into the camera. When the camera is plugged into the PC, turn it on and wait a few moments for Windows 8 to recognize it.

Canon EOS DIGITAL REBEL XTi
Tap to choose what happens with this device.

2 Keep an eye out on the computer screen's upper-right corner. When you see the Tap to Choose What Happens with This Device prompt, click or tap it to open it. (If it disappears, turn off the camera's power, turn it back on again, and wait for the notice.)

3 Choose one of the options that appears. You can import the photos in the Photos app, in File Explorer, or take no action. Windows remembers the choice you make here and repeats it automatically the next time you plug your camera into the computer.

REMEMBER

If Windows 8 doesn't recognize your camera when you plug it in, Windows 8 needs a translator called a *driver* to communicate with your camera. That driver usually comes with your camera's software, either on a CD or DVD or available from the camera maker's website. Run the camera's software to install the needed driver.

Here's a little more detail about your import options:

- **Import Photos and Videos:** Choose this option to import your photos with the Photos app in the Start screen environment. The Photos app opens whenever you connect the camera to it, and after a few moments shows thumbnails of the photos it finds there, all selected for import. Click or tap photos you don't want to import so the check mark in the upper-right corner disappears. Or click or tap Clear Selection to deselect them all; then select just those you want. Edit the filename at the bottom of the screen if desired and then click

or tap Import to copy the photo to your PC. After the files have imported, click or tap the Close button to return to the Photos app.

- **Open Device to View Files:** Prefer to use the Windows Desktop? Then choose this option. It leaves you staring at your camera's contents as a little folder icon inside a File Explorer window, where you can drag your photos to a folder of your choice.

- **Take No Action:** Changed your mind about importing your photos? Click this option to cancel and return later.

Importing photos from a camera via the Photos app

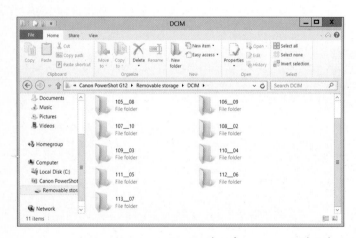

Importing photos from a camera via File Explorer

In the Photos app, you can import photos from a connected camera at any time by clicking or tapping the Import icon from its App bar.

You can also import files from e-mails, thumb drives, websites, and any other mechanism that you would use to download or copy files to your PC. After all, photos are just a type of file. If you place these files in the Pictures library, they'll be visible to the Photos app and other apps that look for photos there.

Working in the Start Screen's Photos App

Windows 8 is designed to favor the Start screen's Photos app, so it launches that app by default when working with photos. The Photos app is designed for showing photos without distraction — perfect for gatherings of friends and family. Plus it lets you see photos stored not just on your PC but also on other PCs and from various websites.

Viewing photos

The simplest way to view photos on your PC is via the Photos app. Open it from the Start screen by clicking or tapping its tile. What you see in the app depends on the images stored on your computer and whether you've connected multiple PCs to the same Microsoft account and enabled file fetching.

Following are the various categories of images that are likely to display. (Windows 8 shows an example photo, if available, in each category's tile.) Note that you may need to scroll to the right to see some of them:

- **Pictures Library:** The Pictures library (including its folders) contains any photos you've saved there. Also stored there are any photos in your camera roll — that is, photos you've taken by using the Camera app on the PC. If you have no photos in either location, you see the words Add Some Photos. ***Note:*** This is the only tile that displays if you don't have an active Microsoft account (that is, if you're using a local account).

- **SkyDrive:** These photos are stored in Microsoft's cloud-based storage service, SkyDrive, if you have a SkyDrive and have uploaded images to it. If your PC can't sign in to SkyDrive (perhaps you have no active Internet connection), an alert appears below the SkyDrive tile. Click or tap the tile to sign in.

- **Devices:** If you have other PCs associated with the same Microsoft account as this PC and have enabled file sharing on them, you see a tile for each. If any of those PCs is unavailable, you see an alert under its name.

- **Facebook Photos:** This tile shows the photos you've uploaded to your Facebook account. If you haven't signed in to Facebook in the Photos app, you see the words See Your Albums; click or tap the tile to sign in.

- **Flickr Photos:** These photos come from your account on Flickr, one of many photo-sharing sites. As with Facebook, click or tap the tile to sign in if you haven't done so previously.

To view a photo, click or tap its category tile. For those categories that have folders, navigate through the folders to the photos you want to view. You can scroll through the photos in a folder or press the Page Up and Page Down keys to navigate through them.

You can use one of these methods to see a photo in full-screen view and then switch back to the folder view of all the photos in that folder:

- Click or tap a photo to see it in full-screen mode. Click or tap the ← icon in the upper-left corner to go back to the available photos.

- Press Ctrl+= to zoom in. Press Ctrl+− to zoom out.

- On a non-touchscreen PC, click the + icon in the lower-right corner to zoom in. (Ignore the Charms bar if it appears.) Click the − to zoom out. These icons don't appear if you have a touchscreen.

- On a touchscreen, use the expand gesture to zoom in to photo at the center of the screen. Use the pinch gesture to zoom out to the folder view.

When viewing a photo from a folder with multiple images, you may also see arrow icons on the sides of the screen that you can click or tap to scroll to the previous or next photo.

When viewing a folder or a photo in it, you can have Photos play a slideshow of that folder's photos by clicking or tapping the Slide Show icon on the App bar. Click or tap the screen to stop the playback.

Set as

View on
SkyDrive

Slide show

Viewing a photo in the Photos app

TIP

You can use the Hide option at the upper right of any tile that isn't signed in to its PC or service to hide a category you don't expect to use. If you do hide a category, you can redisplay it via the Settings charm in Photos; there's a switch in the Photo Settings for each service and PC associated with the same Microsoft account.

TIP

The Settings charm in Photos also has a switch that turns on or off the rotation of the images for each service that displays in Photos. When Shuffle Photos on the App Tile is enabled, the Start screen tile for Photos shows not the standard icon for Photos but an image from one of your libraries, and that image changes periodically. Turn the switch to Off to get the static icon for the tile instead (which can be easier to find).

Deleting photos in the Start screen

When you're viewing folders of photos in the Photos app's Picture Library, you can select photos for deletion. (You can't delete photos from other sources from the Photos app.) To do so, open the App bar and then select the photos to delete:

✔ **To select an individual image,** right-click it or drag it up or down slightly. A light blue border and check mark on the upper-right corner appear, so you know it's selected. To deselect an individual image, right-click it or

drag it up or down slightly; the border and check mark disappear, so you know it's no longer selected.

✔ **To select all images in a folder,** click or tap the Select All icon on the App bar. Click or tap Clear Selection to deselect all photos. ***Note:*** You can't select photos from different sources, such as Pictures Library and SkyDrive.

To delete the selected files, click or tap the Delete icon on the App bar.

For
DUMMIES

Using the Windows Desktop's Pictures Library

Your Pictures library, found on the Navigation pane hugging the left edge of every File Explorer folder, easily earns kudos as the best place in Windows 8 to store your digital photos. When Windows 8 imports your digital camera's photos, it automatically stuffs them there to take advantage of that folder's built-in viewing tools.

Viewing photos

To peek inside any folder in your Pictures library, double-click the folder's icon, and the folder's contents appear.

The Ribbon's View tab works best when you're viewing or organizing photos. Click or tap the View tab and, if you're using a mouse, hover over each option, from Extra Large Icons to Details. As you hover the pointer over an option, the photos change to show you what the view will look like.

The Pictures library's Sort By option offers oodles of ways to sort quickly through thousands of photos by clicking different words, dates, and tags listed on the Sort By menu. The Sort By options include:

- **Date:** This option sorts the photos by the day you added them to your computer, a quick way to find photos added this week.

- **Tags:** If you've added tags — descriptive words — to your photos when importing them from your camera, you can find misplaced photos more easily by sorting them by their tags.

- **Date Taken:** Handy for viewing photos in a timeline, this sorts them by the order you snapped them. This works best when viewing large groups of photos in a single folder.

- **Dimensions:** This option sorts them by physical size, letting you know which ones hog the most disk space. (It's a handy way to find videos you've accidentally taken with your camera.)

By sorting photos in different ways, you can usually ferret out the particular shot you're seeking. The following tips also increase your chances of locating a particular photo:

- Spot a blurred or an ugly photo? Right-click or tap and hold and then choose Delete from the contextual menu that appears. Taking out the garbage makes the good photos easier to find.

- Remember those tags you entered when importing your photos from your camera through the Windows Desktop? Type any photo's tag into the Pictures library's Search box, located in its top-right corner, to have Windows 8 quickly display photos assigned with that particular tag.

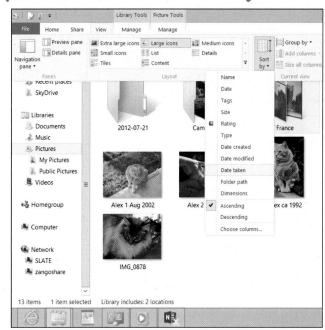

Sorting photos in File Explorer

When viewing a photo, open the App bar and then click or tap the Set As icon. This action opens a menu that lets you use that photo as the image displayed for your choice of Lock Screen, App Tile (the tile that displays for the Photos app in the Start screen), or App Background (the background when you open the Photos app).

- Want to cover your entire desktop with a photo? Right-click or tap and hold the picture and choose Set As Background from the contextual menu that appears. Windows immediately splashes that photo across your desktop.

- Hover your mouse pointer over any photo to see the date it was taken, its rating, size, and dimensions.

Fixing rotated pictures

In the old days, it never mattered how you tilted your camera when taking the photo; you simply turned the printed photo to view it. Many of today's computer screens don't swivel, so Windows 8 rotates the photo for you — if you figure out how.

The trick is to right-click or tap and hold any photo that shows up sideways. Then choose Rotate Clockwise or Rotate Counter Clockwise from the contextual menu.

Viewing a slide show

Windows 8 offers a simple slide slow capability that displays one photo after another. It's not fancy, but it's a built-in way to show photos to friends crowding around your computer screen. Start the photos flowing across the screen in either of these two ways:

✔ When in your Pictures library or folder, go to the Ribbon's Manage tab and then click or tap the Slide Show icon.

✔ When viewing a single photo in the Windows Photo Viewer, click the large, round Play Slide

Show button in the array of controls below the image preview. (To open Photo Viewer, right-click or tap and hold an image and then choose Preview from the contextual menu that appears.)

Either way, Windows immediately darkens the screen, fills the screen with the first picture, and then cycles through each picture in the folder. (If you don't want all the photos in that folder to be in the slide show, select the photos you want to play before starting the slide show.)

Editing Photos Using Paint

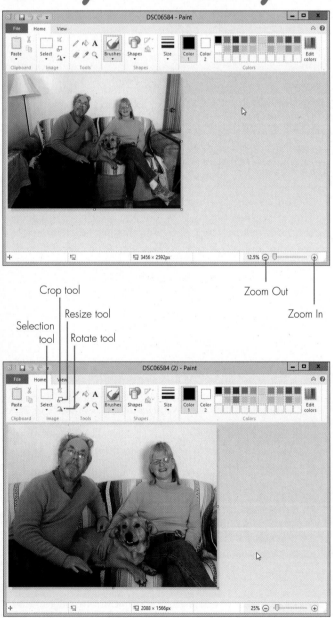

Crop tool

Zoom Out

Resize tool

Zoom In

Selection
tool

Rotate tool

Cropping an image in Paint

There are some great photo-editing tools out there, such as Photoshop Elements, for retouching and otherwise enhancing photos. But if you don't want to spend the money, you can do basic editing in the Paint app that comes with the Windows Desktop.

To be safe, copy any photos you want to work on so you always have the original in case your editing goes horribly wrong.

After launching Paint, press Ctrl+O or click or tap Open from the Ribbon's File tab; then navigate to the file you want to work on. Because Paint opens photos full-sized, you may see only a portion of the photo. In the lower-right corner of the Paint window, click or tap the Zoom Out button (the – icon) or drag the slider to the left. Zoom in and out as necessary to work with different areas of the photo.

Many photos can be improved by *cropping,* which means keeping just part of the photo by cutting out distracting elements. You might crop a photo to concentrate on its most important part. To crop, click or tap the Ribbon's Home tab and then click or tap the Selection tool in the Image section. In the photo, drag a marquee (a selection rectangle) over the area you want to keep — everything outside this area will be deleted. With practice, you can change the area selected by dragging the tiny square handles that appear in each corner and in the middle of each side. When you're happy with the crop area, click or tap the Crop tool. Paint deletes everything outside the selection area.

The other tools that you might find useful in Paint are the Resize and Rotate tools, which are also available in the Image section of the Ribbon's Home tab.

If you're happy with your changes, save the file by pressing Ctrl+S or clicking or tapping the Save button on the Ribbon's File tab.

Sharing Photos

It's great to show people your photos from your computer — when they're in the same room as that computer. But chances are good that you'll want to share your photos with people who aren't always at hand. Plus, sharing them through other services means you have access to duplicate copies of your photos in case your PC gets lost or its hard disk goes kaput.

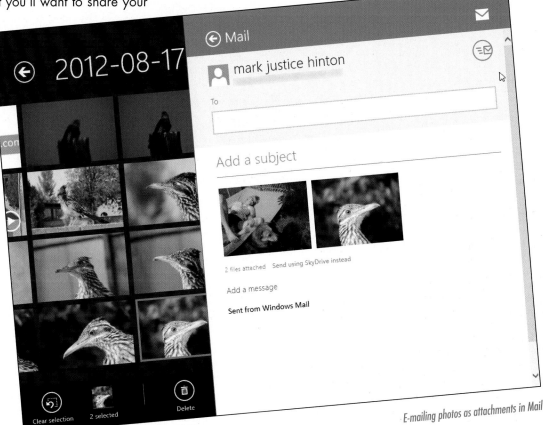

E-mailing photos as attachments in Mail

E-Mailing and Sharing Pictures Online

You can use the Internet to share your photos in two ways: You can send photos via e-mail, or you can upload them to an online service:

- **Uploading photos to an online service:** If you subscribe to a social network service such as Facebook or to a photo-sharing service such as Flickr, upload your photos to them via your browser and the upload controls these services provide on their website to your account. Those you've given access to can then see your pictures.

- **E-mailing photos:** It's easy to e-mail photos. In Mail, Outlook, or whatever e-mail program you use, compose the e-mail and address it the usual way; then use the file-attachment capability to select the files (photos, in this case) you want to send. Then send off the e-mail! Just keep the total size of the attachments to something manageable — many e-mail services won't send or receive e-mails whose attachments total to more than a few megabytes.

Here's how to attach files such as photos in the Start screen's Mail app:

1 Compose your e-mail message as normally.

2 Open the App bar and click or tap the Attachments icon.

3 In the Files screen that appears, navigate to the desired folder or library.

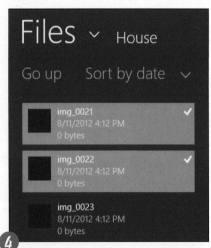

4 Click or tap each desired file to attach; note the check marks that appear next to selected files.

5 Click or tap the Attach button to add them to your e-mail message.

6 Finish composing and addressing your e-mail and then click or tap the Send icon to send it.

TIP

To remove an attachment before sending the e-mail, right-click or tap and hold its preview image in your e-mail; then choose Remove from the contextual menu that appears.

Copying Photos to a CD or DVD

Saving photos to a recordable CD or DVD is a great way to both archive your photos and give them to others, such as a gift for the grandparents of the youngest's birthday party. Follow these steps:

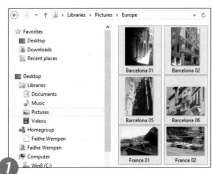

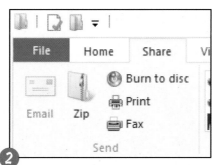

1 Go to the Windows Desktop and open the Pictures library. Select the photos you want to place on a recordable disc.

2 Then go to the Ribbon's Share tab and click or tap Burn to Disc. Windows will ask you to insert a black recordable disc in your DVD drive. (Be sure it can *burn*, or record, CDs and DVDs. For years, most new drives have been able to do so.)

3 Windows then asks how you want the disc to be prepared:

- Select *Like a USB Flash Drive* if you intend for other computers to read the disc. Windows 8 treats the disc much like a folder, letting you copy additional photos to the disc later. It's a good choice when you're backing up only a few pictures, because you can add more to the disc later.

- Select *With a CD/DVD Player* to create discs that play on CD and DVD players attached to TVs. After you write to the disc, it's locked so you can't write to it again.

You're then asked to provide a name for the disc. Do so and then click or tap Next. Click the Burn or Burn to Disc button again, if necessary.

TIP

Don't have enough space on the CD or DVD to hold all your files? Unfortunately, Windows 8 isn't smart enough to tell you when to insert the second disc. Instead, it whines about not having enough room and doesn't burn *any* discs. Try burning fewer files, adding more until you fill up the disc.

REMEMBER

The key to printing nice photos is buying nice (and expensive) photo paper and using a photo-quality printer with the manufacturer's inks. Ask to see printed samples before buying a printer and then buy that printer's recommended photo-quality paper

Printing Pictures

You can print old-fashioned pictures, for adding physical photo albums, placing on refrigerators, and using in Christmas cards. The Windows 8 Photo Printing Wizard offers nearly as many options as the drugstore's photo counter, printing full-page glossies, wallet prints, and nearly anything in between.

To print your photos, follow these steps:

1 Select the photos in the Pictures library.

2 On the Ribbon, go to the Share tab along the top menu and click or tap Print. Or, right-click or tap and hold any of the selected photos and choose Print from the contextual menu that appears.

3 In the Print Pictures window, set your printer, paper size, quality, paper type, photo layout, and the number of times to print each picture. (If you don't set anything, Windows 8 prints one copy of each photo across an expensive sheet of 8½-x-11-inch photo paper.) Make sure you have photo paper in your printer and then click or tap Print.

Here are the options in the Print Pictures window:

- **Printer:** Windows 8 lists your default printer — your only printer, if you have only one — in the top-left menu. If you own a second printer that you use only for photos, choose that printer from the menu.

- **Paper size:** Windows 8 lists paper sizes on this menu in case you want to print on something besides normal 8½-x-11-inch photo paper.

- **Quality:** Leave this set to 600 x 600 dots per inch for most photo printers. If you're printing on a regular printer, set it to 300 x 300 dots per inch.

- **Paper Type:** Select the type of paper you've placed in your printer, usually Photo Paper.

- **Layout:** On the Print Picture window's right edge, choose how Windows 8 should arrange the photos on the page. For example, you can print each photo to fill an entire page, print nine wallet photos, or print something in between. Each time you select an option, the wizard displays a preview of the printed page.

- **Copies of Each Picture:** Choose anywhere from 1 to 99 copies of each picture.

- **Fit Picture to Frame:** Leave this check box selected so Windows 8 fills the entire sheet with the photo. (This option may slightly crop your photo's edge for a better fit. Also, if your photo is low-resolution, this option will make it look blocky.)

TIP

Most photo developers print digital photos with *much* better quality paper and ink than your own printer can accomplish. With the high cost of photo paper and ink cartridges, using photo developers often costs less than printing photos yourself. Check your local photo developer's pricing and ask how you should submit your photos — by CD, via memory card, or over the Internet.

Listening to Music

● *Playing your own music* ● *Creating playlists* ● *Buying more music*

Listening to music is one of those activities that people enjoy in almost any venue: while working, relaxing on the couch or at the beach, commuting, dancing at a party, and so on. For years, computers have been able to play music, both through connected earbuds or headphones and through attached speakers.

Windows 8 carries that musical tradition forward, integrating the ability to play your own music with an online music store where you can buy more to download to your PC.

The Music app

Listening to the Music on Your PC

You can play compatible music — MP3, AAC (MPEG-4), ASF, and WAV files — from the Music app in the Start screen environment or from Windows Media Player in the Windows Desktop. Both play the music stored in your My Music folder in the Music library, and both can play music stored in other locations.

When you first double-click or double-tap a music file in the Windows Desktop's File Explorer, you're asked whether to set Music or Windows Media Player as your default music player. You can still use either player as desired, but the default player is the one that will open when you open a music file from File Explorer.

Playing music through the Music app

When you launch the Music app from the Start screen, the opening screen of the app might make you think that it's is simply a place to buy music from Microsoft's online store, Xbox Music. But the Music app is actually a music player that you can use to listen to your music. The trick is to scroll to the left of the page to see the music files in your My Music folder.

Any compatible files in your My Music folder display in the Music app's albums list. The standard view shows a file for each album and playlist you have. To switch to a view that shows all music sorted by song, album, artist, or playlist, tap the My Music link in the top-left corner.

Understanding the controls

To play an album or song from the My Music screen, click or tap its tile or name and then click the Play button that appears.

At the bottom of the screen, the App bar opens with playback controls: Shuffle, Repeat, Previous, Next, and Pause/Play. The App bar disappears after a few seconds, but you can reopen it at any time by right-clicking on the screen or swiping up from the bottom edge or down from the top edge. A reminder on the controls:

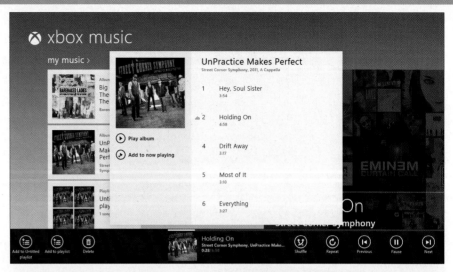

The Music app's standard view of your PC's music (top) and its My Music view, where you can sort music several ways (bottom)

 Shuffle plays the album's or playlist's songs in random order. The icon's background becomes white when Shuffle is enabled.

 Repeat repeats the current playlist or album once all the songs are played. Again, the icon's background becomes white when Repeat is enabled.

 Previous moves to the previous song in the album or playlist, and **Next** moves to the next song.

 Pause halts the playback. The icon becomes **Play**; click or tap it to resume playback.

On the App bar, you'll see an image of the album cover, the name of the current song, its album, its artist, and a timer that shows how far into the song you are.

You don't have to leave the Music app at this current view. Click or tap on the screen to close the controls; if you're viewing the My Music screen, click or tap the ➜ icon to return to the Xbox Music screen.

FOR **DUMMIES**

Controlling playback from the Now Playing view

You can also play music from the opening screen of the Music app — the one that showcases current albums available for purchase at the Microsoft Xbox Music Store. At the bottom-left corner, you see a Now Playing progress bar for the currently playing song, as well as the song's title and artist's name. Click or tap that information to open the Now Playing screen, which puts a collage of album covers in the background and displays the song's title and album in a larger size.

Click or tap the screen to get the basic playback controls: Previous (the < icon), Pause/Play, Next (the > icon), and the scrubber bar. The scrubber bar shows how far into the song you currently are. Click or tap it to reveal the scrubber head, which you can then drag to move to any point in the song.

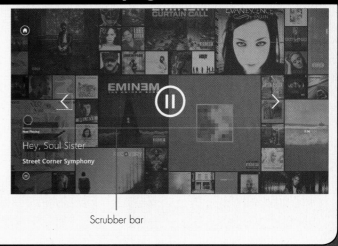

Scrubber bar

If you're playing a song and then switch to another app, the music continues to play. On the Start screen, the Music app's tile shows the current song. To pause or change songs, you must return to the Music app.

To adjust the volume (from any app, not just Music), open the Settings charm and then click or tap the Volume icon at the bottom of the pane. This action opens a volume slider you drag to increase or decrease the volume. Click or tap anywhere to close that slider. PC tablets and some laptops also have physical volume buttons.

TIP

To play a music file not in your My Music folder, open the App bar in the Music app and click or tap the Open File icon; then navigate to the desired music file.

Working with playlists

You're not restricted to organizing your music by songs or albums. Windows supports *playlists,* which are collections of songs you put together yourself — the digital version of the venerable mix tape.

The Music app has a playlist called Now Playing that shows whatever song is currently playing, plus any songs you add to the playlist. As you peruse your music and open albums or click or tap songs in the My Music screen, you can add a song to the Now Playing playlist by clicking or tapping the Add to Now Playing icon that appears.

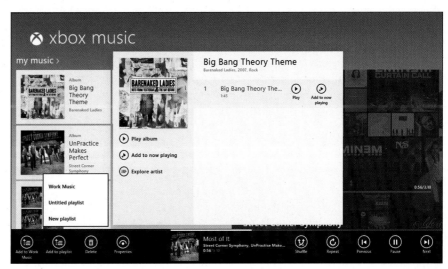

Adding songs to a playlist

But rather than picking and choosing each song every time you listen to music, you probably want to create playlists you can use over and over, such as for parties, road trips, or commuting. To add songs to a playlist, follow these steps:

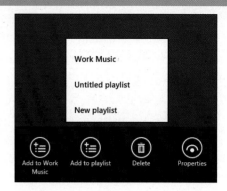

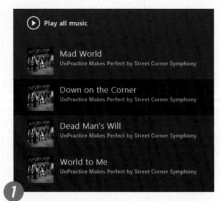

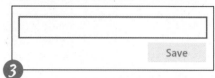

1 Select a song (the entire album is presumed to be your desired selection if you don't select a specific song).

2 Open the App bar by right-clicking or, on a touchscreen, swiping up from the bottom edge or down from the top edge.

3 You have a couple options. (a.) Tap the Add to Playlist icon, which opens a menu showing any existing playlists and the New Playlist option. Tap an existing playlist to add the song or album to it. (b.) Or click or tap New Playlist to create a new playlist and add the music to it. In the dialog box that appears, enter the playlist's name and then click or tap Save to create it.

The most recently used playlist appears in the Music app's main screen (in the My Music section) along with your albums. To play other playlists, you have two choices, depending on where the playlist was created:

✔ **Created in the Music app:** Click or tap the My Music link and then the Playlists link. Click or tap the desired playlist from the tiles that appear.

✔ **Created in Windows Media Player:** Open the App bar and click or tap the Open File icon. Then click or tap the Playlists button in the screen that appears. Click or tap the desired playlist in the list that appears. (See the next section for more on Windows Media Player.)

To remove a song from a Music app's playlist, open the playlist, click or tap the song, and then click the Remove from Playlist icon that appears.

To delete a Music app playlist, open it and click or tap the Delete icon on the App bar. It's that easy, so be careful not to delete a playlist accidentally!

Playing music through Windows Media Player

If you've used earlier versions of Windows, you're likely familiar with Windows Media Player, the Windows Desktop app for playing music and videos. It's still available in Windows 8, and it works just as it did in Windows 7.

Windows Media Player shows any music in your My Music folder, organized by album (the default setting). But you can change the sorting using the Artist, Album, and Genre options in the Navigation pane at left, and you can change how the songs sort by clicking the desired title option, such as Rating or Title.

Here's how to play your music in Media Player:

✔ **To play a song,** double-click or double-tap it. At the bottom of the Windows Media Player window, you can find several playback controls: Shuffle, Repeat, Stop, Previous, Play/Pause, Next, and Volume. They work just like the similar controls in the Start screen app.

▶ **To create playlists** in Windows Media Player, click or tap the Create Playlist button on the toolbar and then enter the playlist name in the field that opens in the Navigation pane, under the Playlists item. Then drag music files into that playlist in the Navigation pane to add them.

▶ **To play a playlist,** just tap the playlist. While a playlist is playing, you can add songs to it by dragging them into the Play pane that appears at right.

▶ **To delete a song from a playlist,** open the playlist so the Play pane appears, select the song to remove, and press Delete — not Backspace. (To access the Delete key on a touchscreen keyboard, open the full keyboard.)

Playlists created in the Music app aren't available to Windows Media Player.

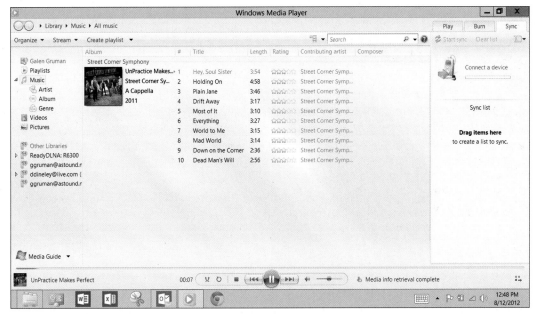

Playing songs in Windows Media Player

Buying Music Online

The Music app and Windows Media Player both let you buy music from Microsoft's online store, though the Music app is much more focused on enticing you to do so.

To buy music, you must be signed in to your Microsoft account or your Xbox Live account. Both apps automatically connect to that account if you've signed in elsewhere.

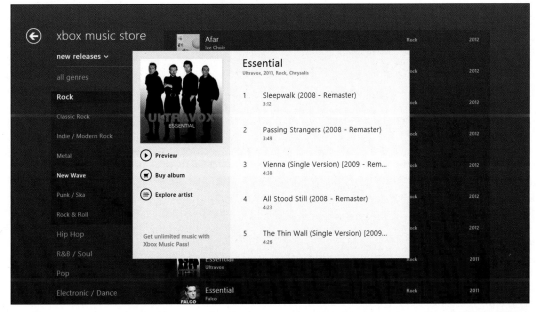

Buying music in the Music app

In the Music app, scroll through the panes — Xbox Music Store (where you can sort music by genre, new releases, and other criteria) and Most Popular — to see whether anything catches your interest.

Click an album's tile to get more details and then use the buttons to buy the album, preview a song (which plays it on your PC), or play the album on your Xbox (if you have an Xbox Music account). Click outside the album preview to close it.

You can manage your account, check past purchases, redeem credits, and manage your billing options in the Music app's Settings charm, in its Accounts pane.

In Windows Media Player, it's not as easy to buy music, so the Music app is a better option. If you insist on buying music through Windows Media Player, note the Shop link

that appears below the album icon in the Play pane as music is playing. Click it to open the Microsoft music store and then navigate it to choose the music you want to buy. What makes this difficult is that the online store doesn't fit well onscreen in Windows Media Player, so it can be hard to navigate.

You can buy music online from other stores, not just Microsoft's. Just make sure the files are in a compatible format and not copy-protected, so they can play in Music or Windows Media Player.

Importing your CDs into your PC

In a process known as *ripping*, Windows Media Player can copy your CDs to your PC as MP3 files, the industry standard for digital music. But until you tell the player that you want MP3 files, it creates *WMA* files — a format that won't play on iPods, or many other music players.

To make Windows Media Player create songs with the more versatile MP3 format instead of WMA, and then copy a CD to your PC's hard drive, follow these steps:

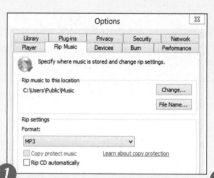

1 Click or tap the Organize button in the top-left corner of the Windows Media Player window, click Options, and click the Rip Music tab. Choose MP3 instead of WMA from the Format menu and nudge the audio quality over a tad from 128 to 256 or even 320 for better sound.

2 Open Windows Media Player, insert a CD into your PC, and click or tap the Rip CD button in Windows Media Player.

The app connects to the Internet, identifies your CD, and fills in the album's name, artist, and song titles. Then it begins copying the CD's songs to your PC and listing their titles in the Windows Media Player library. That's it! Well, unless it can't identify the CD, in which case, proceed to Step 3.

3 Right-click or tap and hold the first track in the list of songs and choose Find Album Info.

If you're connected to the Internet, type the album's name into the Search box and then click or tap Search. If the Search box finds your album, select its name, click or tap Next, and click Finish.

If you're not connected to the web or the Search box comes up empty, right-click or tap and hold the first song, click or tap Edit, and enter the song title. Repeat this process for the other songs' titles, album, artist, genre, and year tags.

Windows Media Player automatically places your ripped CDs into your Music library.

Watching Videos

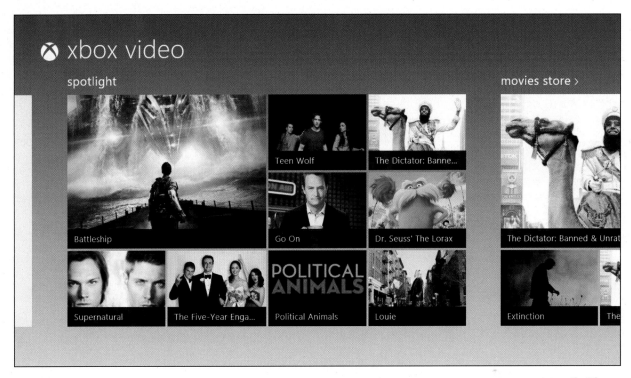

xbox video

spotlight

movies store >

Teen Wolf

The Dictator: Banne...

Battleship

Go On

Dr. Seuss' The Lorax

The Dictator: Banned & Unrat

Supernatural

The Five-Year Enga...

POLITICAL ANIMALS

Political Animals

Louie

Extinction

The

The Video app

Watching movies and TV shows on a computer is a popular activity. It's very common for college students, whose dorm rooms often don't have much space for TVs, so the computer doubles as a TV. But as anyone who travels knows, watching movies — commercial offerings or home videos — on a tablet or laptop in flight or in a hotel room is a great way to while away your downtime, and it usually beats the selections available in airplanes and hotels.

The Windows 8 apps for watching videos are very similar to its apps for listening to music, so if you know how to use one, you pretty much know how to use the other. And on the Windows Desktop, you use the same app for both music and video: Windows Media Player.

REMEMBER

Windows 8 no longer plays DVDs; you must buy the Media Center Pack upgrade available only for Windows 8 Pro to watch DVDs on it. You also need the Media Center Pack to play any MPEG-1 and MPEG-2 video files you may have. You can upgrade Windows 8 to Windows 8 Pro so you can get the Media Center Pack, but you can't upgrade Windows RT to Windows 8 Pro, so PC tablets using Windows RT cannot play DVDs or MPEG-1 or MPEG-2 video files.

Watching Movies and TV Shows

You can play compatible video files — such as MPEG-4 files — from the Video app in the Start screen environment or from the Windows Media Player on the Windows Desktop. Both play the videos stored in your My Videos folder in the Video library, and both can play videos stored in other locations.

Playing video through the Video app

Just as the Music app appears to be just a front end to Microsoft's music store, the Video app appears to be a front end to Microsoft's video store. But as with the Music app, you can play any compatible videos — those in the MP4 (MPEG-4), ASF, or AVI formats — stored in your My Videos folder by scrolling to the left of the opening screen.

If you click My Videos, you can switch the view to show all videos organized by Movies, TV shows, or Other (such as videos you create or download from the web). The videos are sorted by duration, title, or date added.

TIP

To watch YouTube or other web-based videos, go to the desired website in your browser.

REMEMBER

When you first double-click or double-tap a video file in File Explorer, you're asked whether to set Video or Windows Media Player as your default video player. You can still use either player as desired, but the default player is the one that will open when you open a video file from File Explorer.

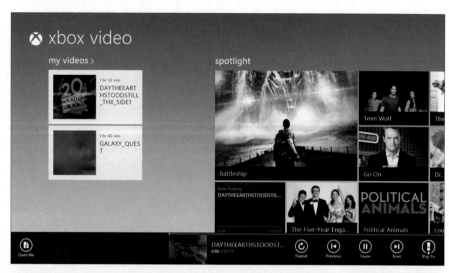

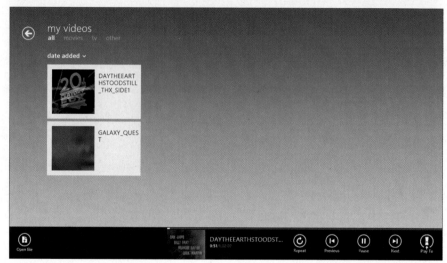

The Video app's standard view of your PC's videos (top) and its My Videos view, where you can sort videos several ways (bottom)

To play a video, click or tap its tile or name — that's all it takes.

For a few seconds, playback controls appear onscreen; click or tap the screen to reveal them at any time. You can also open the App bar to display playback controls. The onscreen controls offer just the Play/Pause button and the scrubber head, which you can drag to move within the video. The App bar provides those controls plus the Previous, Next, and Repeat icons.

When you switch away from the video playback window, the video keeps playing. In the Video app, you can see a thumbnail of the video's current scenes on the App bar. If you move to the main Video app screen, which shows the featured video rentals and

purchases at the Windows Store, the bottom-left tile shows a preview of the current video, using either its preview icon or, if none is available, the first scene in the video. On the Start screen, the Video app's tile shows the name of the current video.

To pause or change videos, you must return to the Video app.

To adjust the volume (from any app, not just Video), open the Settings charm and then click or tap the Volume icon at the bottom of the pane. This action opens a volume slider you drag to increase or decrease the volume. Click or tap anywhere to close that slider. PC tablets and some laptops also have physical volume buttons.

FOR DUMMIES

TIP

To play a video file not in your My Videos folder, open the App bar in the Video app and click or tap the Open File icon; then navigate to the desired video file.

DAYTHEEARTHSTOODSTILL_THX_SIDE1

Now Playing   0:07/1:32:07

Repeat   Previous   Pause   Next   Play To

Playing video through Windows Media Player

Windows Media Player shows any videos in your My Videos folder, organized by title (the default setting). But you can change the sorting by using the labels above the video list: Title, Length, Release Year, Genre, Actors, Rating, Size, and Parental Rating.

Double-click or double-tap a video to play it in the playback window that appears. Enlarge the window to see the movie in a more comfortably large frame and then click or tap the window to get the playback controls: Shuffle, Repeat, Previous, Play/Pause, Next, and Volume.

Playing videos in Windows Media Player

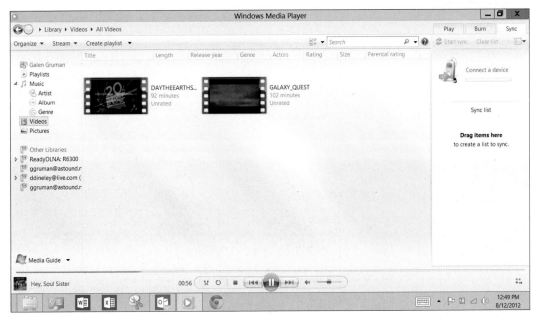

Seeing available videos in Windows Media Player

Buying Movies and TV Shows

The Video app lets you buy or rent videos from Microsoft's online store, something you can't do through Windows Media Player.

To buy or rent videos, you must be signed in to your Microsoft account or your Xbox Live account. The Video app automatically connects to that account if you've signed in elsewhere.

In the Video app, scroll through the panes such as Movies Store and Television Store to see if anything piques your interest, and click or tap a tile if it does. Otherwise, click or tap a link such as Movies Store or Television Store to open a screen that lets you narrow down video suggestions by genre, last night's TV shows, free videos, TV networks, movie studios, and recent releases.

Click or tap a movie or TV show's tile to get more details. For a TV show, click or tap View Seasons to see available seasons for the show, and click the desired season to go to its details screen. On the details screen, click or tap the Buy or Rent button to purchase or rent the show. You'll see the price only after clicking or tapping, but don't worry: You have to confirm the transaction before actually being charged.

You can manage your account, check past purchases, redeem credits, and manage your billing options in the Video app's Settings charm, in its Accounts pane.

Buying a movie in the Video app (top) and buying a season of a TV show (bottom)

You can buy movies and TV shows online from other stores, not just Microsoft's. Just make sure the files are in a compatible format and not copy-protected, so they will play in Video or Windows Media Player.

Burning CDs and DVDs

To create a music CD with your favorite songs, you can create a playlist containing those songs, listed in the order you want to play them. Then insert a blank recordable CD into your PC and click or tap the Ribbon's Burn tab in Windows Media Player. Take up the player's offer to import your current playlist and then click or tap the Start Burn button.

But what if you want to duplicate a CD, perhaps to create a disposable copy of your favorite CD to play in your car? Or make copies of your kids' CDs before they create pizzas out of them?

Unfortunately, Windows 8 has no Duplicate CD option. Instead, you must jump through the following hoops to create a new CD with the same songs in the same fidelity as the original CD.

Burning music to a CD from a burn list in Windows Media Player

Music and Video

Follow these steps to create a new CD:

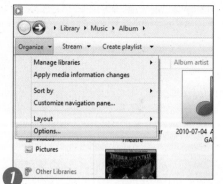

1 In Windows Media Player, click or tap the Ribbon's Organize tab and then click Options.

2 Click or tap the Rip Music tab, change the Format box to WAV (Lossless), and click OK. Then insert a blank recordable CD into your CD drive.

3 In Windows Media Player's Navigation pane, click or tap the Music category and choose Album to see your saved CDs.

4 Right-click or tap and hold the album in your library and then choose Add To➜Burn List from the contextual menu that appears. If your burn list already has some listed music, click or tap the Clear List button to clear it and then add your CD's music to the burn list.

5 Click or tap the Start Burn button.

A simpler solution is to buy CD-burning software from your local office supply or computer store. Unlike Windows Media Player, most CD-burning programs have a Duplicate CD button for one-click convenience.

The process for importing and burning DVDs is much harder, requiring special software to do so, such as Roxio's suite of tools (**www.roxio.com**). Many people like to copy their commercial DVDs for viewing on their computers, but tools such as Roxio's won't do that, for fear of violating copyright restrictions.

In the United States, it's perfectly legal to copy music and videos you've bought, as long as it's for your own personal use, but it's illegal for software makers to provide the tools to break the copy protection. But the French company HandBrake (**www.handbrake.fr**) isn't subject to U.S. law, and its HandBrake software lets you import your commercial DVDs for playback on your PC. Just be sure to honor the law and keep those copies for personal use, such as for playback on airplane trips.

Getting to Know Settings

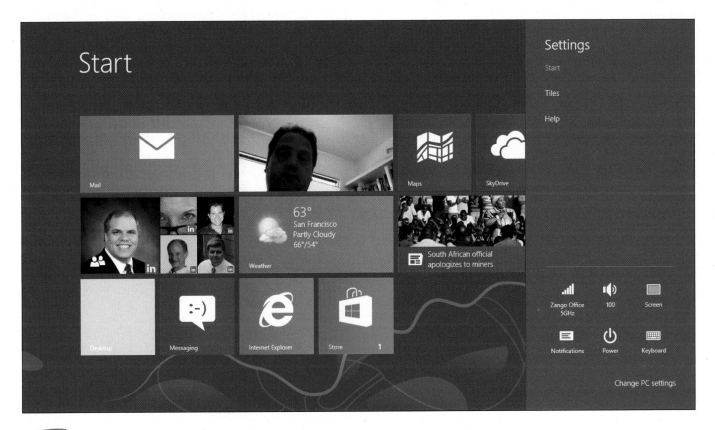

Everybody is different. And if you look at their computers, you'll find that they're often different as well, with different icon arrangements, folder names, applications, and personalization settings. After all, a PC is a *personal computer*, which means it's adjusted to meet the needs and preferences of its user.

Windows 8 has two primary locations where you set the preferences for how you prefer to work, as well as to configure how your PC itself and its peripherals (monitor, keyboard, printer, mouse, network, and so on) work. One is the PC Settings screen, accessible from the Charms bar whether you are in the Start screen or Windows Desktop, and the other is the Control Panel, which you access from the Windows Desktop.

The PC Settings screen and the Control Panel have some overlap — setting up a new peripheral in one sets it up in the other. But other preference controls, such as for screen resolution, are just for the one environment. The Control Panel also has many more controls than PC Settings, most of which (but not all) are focused on the Windows Desktop.

Using the Easy-Access Settings

The Settings charm, which you can open from the Start screen and Windows Desktop, always shows six options at the bottom that provide quick access to commonly used controls:

✔ **Networks:** The currently connected network is displayed, if you're connected to a network. Click or tap the icon to see a list of available networks you can connect to. You can also enable Airplane Mode, which turns off all radios on the PC so it can be used safely in flight.

✔ **Volume:** This shows the speakers' current volume level. Click or tap it to open a slider to adjust the volume.

✔ **Screen:** Click or tap this icon to open a slider to adjust the screen's brightness. There's also a button above the slider that disables or enables screen rotation on a tablet; you can also press ⊞+O to toggle rotation on or off. A lock appears on the Screen icon in the Settings charm when rotation is locked.

✔ **Notifications:** Click or tap this icon to open a menu that lets you disable all notifications for your choice of one hour, three hours, or eight hours.

✔ **Power:** Click or tap this icon to open a menu that lets you put the PC to sleep, shut it down, or restart it.

✔ **Keyboard:** Click or tap this icon to open a menu where you can open onscreen keyboards for other languages (if you have set any up) as well as the handwriting-recognition "keyboard." To open a different keyboard, tap and hold on the desired option for a second or two. If your PC has only one keyboard, the icon won't respond to a click. (All touchscreen devices have at least two keyboards: your default language keyboard plus the handwriting keyboard.)

At the top of the Settings charm are options for the currently open app (or for the Start screen, if it's displayed). At the bottom is the Change PC Settings link.

For the Start screen itself, you have just a couple configuration options in its Settings charm, and you can access them both by clicking the Tiles link at the top of the Settings charm:

✔ Set the Show Administrative Tools switch to On to have tiles for these expert controls available in Start screen.

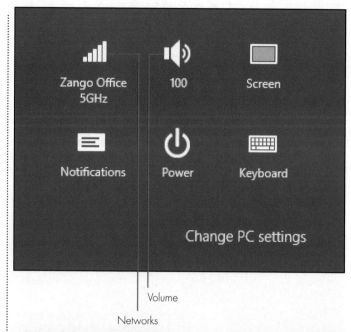

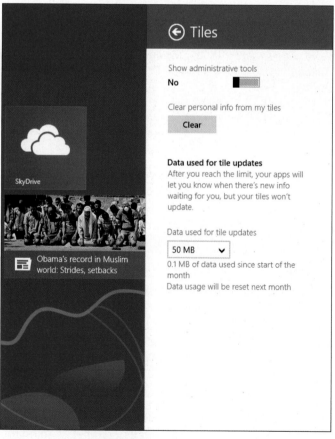

✔ Click the Clear option to remove all personal information from live app tiles — this essentially sets them so they no longer display current information in the Start screen, such as your current photo roll, e-mail messages, and local weather.

On the Windows Desktop, the options at the top of the Settings charm provide quick access to the Control Panel. Click or tap the Control Panel link to open the Control Panel, click the Personalization link to open the Personalization control panel, or click the PC Info link to open the System control panel.

The options available for each pane in the PC Settings screen and in the Control Panel may vary from device to device based on the features each supports. Typically, features not supported by the current device don't display at all or are grayed out to indicate they aren't applicable.

Configuring via the PC Settings Screen

Most of the time, you'll use the PC Settings screen to customize your PC. It's available in a snap by opening the Settings charm and then clicking or tapping the Change PC Settings link at the bottom. You get 14 panes to choose from in the list at left:

Personalize

Here, you set the background images for the lock screen and Start screen, the photo used for your account, and the apps that can display their status in the lock screen.

Users

Here, you switch accounts, set or change your password, and add user accounts.

Notifications

Use this pane to enable notifications, which briefly appear in both the Start screen and Windows Desktop in the upper right-corner of the screen; click or tap them to open the app issuing the notification. You can also set Windows 8 to

play a sound for such alerts and display them in the lock screen. Finally, the Notifications pane shows all apps that can issue notifications, with an On/Off switch for each to control those that you want to get notifications from.

Search

In this pane, you set which apps appear in the Search charm by using their On/Off switches. You also control whether Windows tracks your search history. Search history has two

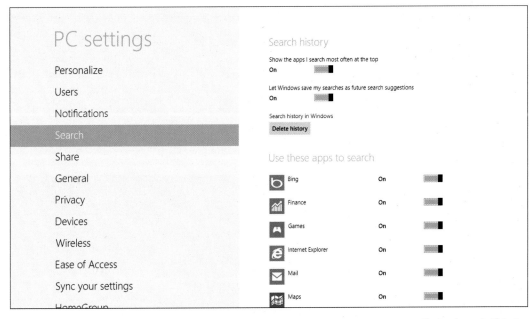

The Search pane in PC Settings

components, each of which has its own On/Off switch. One orders the items in the Search charm based on how often you search them, and the other tracks your search results to use them in the future when you search for the same or similar items.

Share

Here, you set which apps appear in the Share charm for sharing content; use the On/Off switches to enable or disable sharing through them. In the Frequent section, there's one On/Off switch to put at the top of the share list the apps you use most frequently to share with. Another On/Off switch controls whether a list displays of how you share most often; you also can set how many items appear in that list. The two lists are very similar, so you may find you can turn one off.

General

This pane has a lot of controls:

- **Time:** Use the Time section to set the current time zone and whether to adjust automatically for Daylight Savings Time.

- **App Switching:** The App Switching section enables or disables the use of the ⊞ key to switch between the current and last-used app, as well as enables the swipe gesture from the left side of the screen to open the last-used app.

- **Touch Keyboard:** This section controls how the onscreen keyboard works. You can enable or disable the display of suggested corrections as you type, the insertion of a space after selecting a suggested word, automatically adding a period when you type two spaces, automatically capitalizing the first word in a sentence, entering Caps Lock mode when double-tapping the Shift key, playing a sound as you tap each key, and enabling the full-keyboard option for the onscreen keyboard.

- **Spelling:** In this section, you can set Windows 8 to auto-correct misspelled words as you type and to highlight words it suspects are misspelled as you type.

- **Screen:** The one option here enables a PC to automatically adjust screen brightness based on how much light is in the room. (It uses its camera to sense that light, so PCs with no cameras don't offer this setting.)

- **Language:** Click or tap Language Preferences to open the Language control panel on the Windows Desktop, where you can add languages that Windows provides onscreen controls and supports local keyboards for, such as in a multilingual environment.

- **Available Storage:** Click or tap View App Sizes to see how much space each app is taking on your PC. This setting can be useful if you're running out of space and want to see whether little-used apps might free up enough space if uninstalled (which you do in the Start screen or via the Programs control panel on the Windows Desktop).

- **Refresh Your PC without Affecting Your Files:** Click or tap Get Started to reinstall Windows without deleting your data files to try to eliminate any oddities that may be affecting performance.

- **Remove Everything and Reinstall Windows:** Click or tap Get Started to erase the hard disk and reinstall Windows from scratch.

- **Advanced Startup:** Click Restart to open a screen where you can choose to restart as is, troubleshoot your PC (including changing its startup options), or shut down. If you click or tap Troubleshoot, a new screen opens that lets you refresh the PC, reset it, or open advanced options such as enabling Safe Mode.

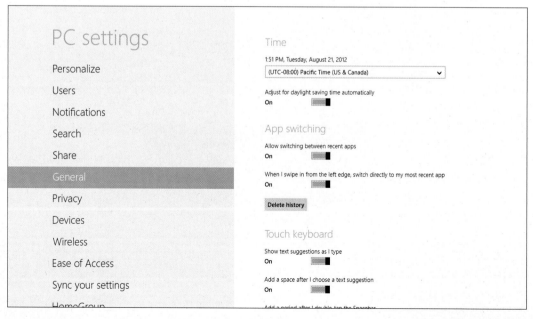

The General pane in PC Settings

Devices

Use this pane to add and delete peripherals such as printers and keyboards.

Wireless

Use this pane's controls to turn off all radios (Airplane Mode) so the PC is safe to use in flight. You can also enable specific radios, such as Wi-Fi and cellular (3G or LTE). Turning off radios when not needed can conserve battery life.

Ease of Access

Three controls here help make Windows easier to use if you have weak sight: High Contrast, Make Everything on Your Screen Bigger, and Cursor Thickness. You also can set what pressing ⊞+Volume Up activates: nothing, the Magnifier (which magnifies the text under it as you move it across the screen), Narrator (which speaks the names of items and controls onscreen), or the onscreen keyboard. The Magnifier and Narrator options are useful if you're visually impaired; the Onscreen Keyboard option is a nice convenience for anyone. The final option, Show Notifications For, controls how long notifications display in the upper-right corner of the screen.

Sync Your Settings

If you're using a Microsoft account, you can sync the settings on one PC to all other PCs signed in to the same account. This synchronization is on by default, but you can turn it off or back on here. You also can adjust which settings are synced in the list below; all are on by default. Finally, at the very bottom are two options for syncing over a metered connection, such as a cellular connection. You can turn off syncing over metered connections entirely or just when roaming; the right choice depends on whether your carrier limits you to a specific amount of data usage on its network (most do) or just when you're roaming on other networks.

HomeGroup

Click or tap the Create option to enable simple sharing with other users on your local network.

Windows Update

Windows 8 automatically installs updates to Windows and its antivirus software, Windows Defender. You can force a check for new updates by clicking or tapping Check for Updates Now. If there are updates available, you see

The Ease of Access pane in PC Settings

blue text in the paragraph above that button (the wording varies); click or tap it to see the details of what's available and, optionally, install it immediately rather than wait for Windows 8 to do it on its normal schedule.

TIP

If you use the Search charm and click or tap the Settings icon, you can search the Start screen apps' settings and all the Windows Desktop control panels, Action Center troubleshooters, help entries, and much more for what you're seeking help with. (The Action Center is a control panel in the System and Security group that helps you troubleshoot problems on your PC.)

Configuring via Control Panel

The Control Panel on the Windows Desktop should be familiar to anyone who's used earlier versions of Windows — Microsoft has used the Control Panel for years to let users personalize their PCs and manage hardware, security, and other aspects of Windows.

Because there are dozens and dozens of controls, only some of which any one individual will want to change, you should set aside a couple hours on a rainy day and just go through each control panel to see whether an option looks like something you'd want to adjust. The control panel groups that are most likely to have aspects you'd want to adjust are

- Appearance and Personalization
- Clock, Language, and Region
- Default Programs control panel in the Programs group

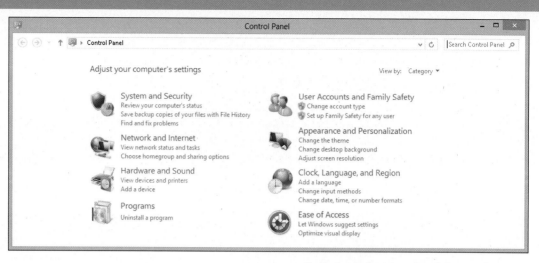

The Windows Desktop's Control Panel, showing its home screen

You can open the Control Panel in several ways:

- In the Settings charm in either the Start screen or the Windows Desktop, click or tap Control Panel. (To jump straight to the Personalization control panel, click or tap Personalization; to jump straight to the System control panel, click or tap PC Info.)
- In the Start screen, type **control panel** and then click or tap it in the search results pane that appears. (You need a physical keyboard to do this search.)
- In either the Windows Desktop or Start screen, press ⊞+X to open the Power User menu and then choose Control Panel.

The Control Panel has eight main groups of controls. Click or tap the desired group or a link to a specific function within that group. Use the ← and → icons at the upper left of the Control Panel window to navigate back and forth through the control panels you've visiting (as if it were a browser whose web pages you were traversing). Use the ↑ icon to move up a level in the Control Panel hierarchy. When you open a Control Panel group, a list of specific control panels appears in its left side; click or tap a link to go to that specific control panel. Click or tap the Control Panel Home link on the left to get back to the main Control Panel window's list of groups.

Here's what the eight Control Panel groups offer:

- **System and Security:** The 11 control panels here mix a variety of features. Many are related to security and troubleshooting. As for the few others, use Power Options to enable power-savings mode if desired, choose when to turn off the monitor after the computer has been idle, and determine when to put the computer to sleep after it's been idle.

TIP

Consider pinning the Control Panel to the Windows Desktop's taskbar so it's readily accessible in that environment.

- **Network and Internet:** The three control panels here let you manage your local network (including Wi-Fi connections), your Homegroup, and the settings for the Internet Explorer 10 browser.
- **Hardware and Sound:** The nine control panels here manage the internal and external hardware for your PC: printers, monitors, speakers, microphones, CD and DVD drives, pen input and touchscreen gestures, and location detection.
- **Programs:** This control panel is where you can remove or modify Windows Desktop apps. It's also where you can set what happens when you insert DVDs, CDs, USB thumb drives, or other storage media to the PC. For various file types, you can specify that they're always opened in a specific app, that nothing happens, or that you're asked what to do. You can also set which applications are the default for specific file types — use this control panel to favor Start screen apps or Windows Desktop apps (as you prefer) consistently in Windows 8.

User Accounts and Family Safety: The User Accounts control panel's Change User Account Type option lets you assign a user as an administrator (if your current account also has administrator rights), which gives that person full control over the PC. The first person who sets up an account has administrator rights by default; everyone else has standard rights, which limits them to controls over just their files and account. (You add new user accounts from the PC Settings screen, not in the Control Panel.) The Manage Another Account option lets you change the administrator rights for another user or delete that account, as well as apply Family Safety controls to it.

Appearance and Personalization: The six control panels here let people customize the Windows Desktop to match their personalities and readability needs:

Personalization: You can set the desktop background, colors of window borders, size of menus and other window items, and sounds that play (or not) for specific alerts and actions (such as closing an app).

Display: You can adjust the size of text in all Windows Desktop windows, as well as change the screen resolution (which can fit more items on the screen but make them all smaller, or make everything bigger but allow fewer items to be onscreen at the same time).

Taskbar: You can set how control and notification icons display on the taskbar: not at all, always the icon, or only when there's a notification to you.

Folder Options: You can hide file extensions (such as .exe for programs and .docx for Word files) in File Explorer, and it lets you specify whether files open with a double-click (or double-tap) or with a single click (or tap) in File Explorer.

Fonts: You can add fonts to Windows for use by all Windows Desktop apps.

Ease of Access: This control panel is explained later.

Clock, Language, and Region: These control panels are ones you'll use rarely after your initial setup.

Date and Time: You can set the date, time, and time zone, and you can add more clocks so you can see multiple time zones at a glance.

Language: You can tell Windows which languages you want it to work in so you can use keyboards and menus in the desired languages.

Region: You can tell Windows which region's settings to use for dates (such as **10/26/2012**

The Appearance and Personalization control panel group (top) and the Clock, Language, and Region control panel group (bottom)

for Oct. 26, 2012 in the United States versus **26/10/2012** in Europe) and numerals (such as **1.5** for the decimal point in the United States and **1,5** in Europe).

Ease of Access Center: This group lets you set display magnification, visual cues, text-to-speech narration, speech recognition, and input device settings to help the visual-, hearing- and motor-impaired.

Working with Hardware

● *Adding hardware in the Start screen* ● *Setting up hardware from the Windows Desktop*

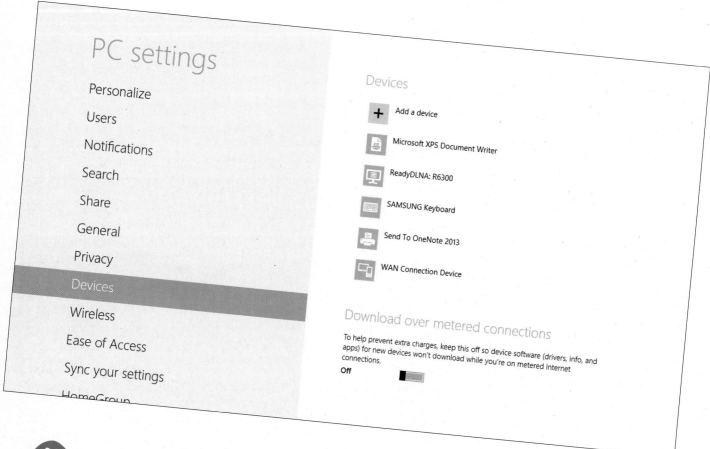

Chances are good that your PC isn't completely self-sufficient: You've added a keyboard, mouse, and monitor and probably also connected to a printer. You likely have some USB sticks or other memory cards. Even if you own a PC tablet, you probably connect to at least some of these hardware devices some of the time, such as to get a larger screen, a physical keyboard, and a mouse when "docked" at your desk.

Windows auto-detects a lot of hardware — plug it in and it just works. That's typical for mice, monitors, storage devices, and keyboards. Some devices, such as printers, need special software called *drivers* that tell Windows how to use them, and if Windows recognizes the device and has an Internet connection, it often can get those drivers on its own and set up the devices without your assistance.

Most of the time, all you have to do is turn on the device and connect the hardware to your computer, such as via a cable to the USB port (the most common port used to connect devices to PCs). If the device uses Bluetooth or other wireless technology, make sure its wireless radio is on.

When that doesn't work, you may need to install the drivers manually and then connect the device to the computer. If a disc came with the hardware, you can install the drivers from that disc. If not, you can download the drivers from the manufacturer's website and then install them by double-clicking the installation file in your My Documents folder or wherever you downloaded them to (so you need to be on the Windows Desktop to do this). But in many cases, you won't have to do that work.

But what do you do if you connect a device, even after installing the driver, and the PC still doesn't see it as connected? First, try to use the Settings charm:

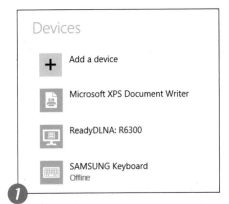

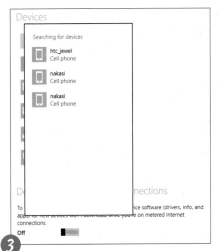

1 Go to the Settings charm's PC Settings screen and open its Devices pane. A list of devices appears.

2 If the device is listed but its label says "Offline," turn it off and then back on to see whether that connects it. If not, try restarting the PC. After that, if the device is still listed as disconnected, right-click or tap and hold its name; then click or tap the – icon that appears to the right of its name to delete it. Turn off the device, make sure it is connected or its wireless is on, and turn it back on.

3 If the device isn't visible at all in the device list, click or tap Add a Device. If the device appears in the list that appears, click or tap it to install it.

If you can't get the device to show as connected in the Settings charm, it's time to try using the Control Panel instead:

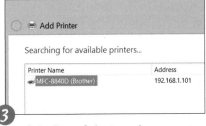

1 Go to the Windows Desktop, open the Control Panel, and in the Hardware and Sound group, click or tap Devices and Printers.

2 Click or tap Add a Device (or Add a Printer if you're adding a printer).

3 If the list of devices that appears includes your device, click or tap its name and then click Next. If Windows can't find the driver, it asks whether you want to try to download it from Windows Update or use a disc that has the drivers. Click the appropriate option and follow the prompts to install the driver. If necessary, go to the manufacturer's website to see whether you can download the needed driver. If so, download and install it. If not, contact the company for help.

REMEMBER

Some network devices, such as printers, may not display in the list of recognized hardware, either in the PC Settings screen or in the Control Panel. If you can, try connecting them directly to the PC via a USB or other cable (the needed cable almost always is included with the device) so the PC "sees" them. After that, the device is usually visible via the network. But if not, ask the manufacturer for help.

WARNING!

The Device Manager control panel lets you update drives and see a detailed list of all hardware inside and connected to your PC. This is an expert feature that you should use only with care.

Using the Devices charm

You may have noticed a charm named Devices on the Charms bar. If you opened it, chances are good that you saw only the Second Screen option, realized you have only one monitor, and moved on. Like all the other charms, the Devices charm shows only items that pertain to the app that's currently open. So, if you see only the Second Screen option, that just means it is the only device-related action your PC can take in that current app (including the Windows Desktop and Start screen).

But if you open an app that can use other devices, you see them listed. For example, the Devices charm for the Start screen's Internet Explorer app shows any connected printers. It also shows the virtual printer Microsoft XPS

Document Writer, which creates a PDF-like file of your printout that you can view onscreen. If you have Office 2013 installed, an option labeled Send to OneNote 2013 also appears; clicking or tapping it sends the virtual printout to that note-taking app.

Just click or tap the option for the device you want to use, and Windows 8 opens a pane that shows that device's options.

Remember: The Devices charm does not provide access to devices in any Windows Desktop app. Instead, you use an app's traditional controls, such as File→Print or the Ribbon's controls, to access devices.

The Devices charm is where you print from when using Start screen apps, via its Print pane

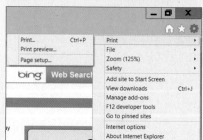

Printing from the Devices charm for a Start screen app (top) and via the Print menu in the Windows Desktop (bottom), here for Internet Explorer

DUMMIES

Making Windows More Accessible

Not everyone has the same abilities, and the folks at Microsoft who created Windows know that. So they've provided some ways to adjust Windows to work better if you have different abilities than most. For example, you can make the screen and its objects larger to help deal with near-sightedness. You can have Windows talk you through screen options if you're visually impaired. You can have Windows use visual alerts rather than sounds if your hearing is impaired. And you can adjust how the mouse and keyboard work to help control the PC despite having arthritis or other motor issues.

As in most cases in Windows 8, some of these settings reside on the Start screen, and some reside on the Windows Desktop. In both environments, the controls are grouped under the Ease of Access label.

The Start Screen's Ease of Access Settings

In the Start screen, there are just a few settings — all in PC Settings' Ease of Access pane — that you can use to make the Start screen more accessible. Note these features may not work on a PC tablet, even if the options are available.

The four accessibility options are

- **High Contrast:** Set this switch to On to invert the screen colors, so Windows runs with a

The Ease of Access Center in the Control Panel

black background, which can make the text and other objects more discernable. Note that this control applies to both the Start screen and the Windows Desktop.

- **Pressing Windows + Volume Up Will Turn On:** From this menu, choose Magnifier if you want the ⊞+Volume Up shortcut to open the magnifier, which enlarges the area around your pointer. Choose Narrator if you want that shortcut to cause Windows to start speaking what's displayed onscreen. Note the Volume Up button may be on your computer, monitor, or keyboard (or more than one) and that Windows may not recognize the Volume Up button on all devices.

- **Make Everything on Your Screen Bigger:** Set this switch to On to enlarge the Start screen. Note that in many apps, screens that normally show two panes will be broken into two screens, and you use the ← icon to get back to the first in the pair.

✔ **Cursor Thickness:**
Change this value to a greater numeral to thicken the cursor that indicates your location when clicking or tapping in a text field in a Start screen or Windows Desktop app.

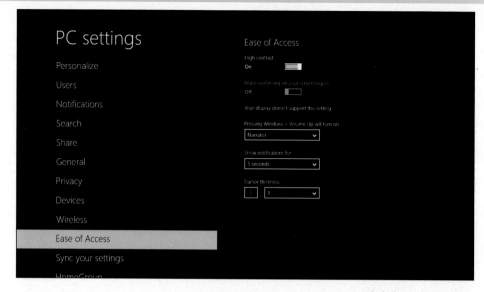

The high-contrast view

The Windows Desktop's Ease of Access Settings

The bulk of accessibility settings in Windows 8 reside where they have long resided in Windows: in the Control Panel's Ease of Access group.

The best way to use its many options is to click or tap Let Windows Suggest Settings in the Ease of Access group. Fill out the quiz that asks you about your eyesight, hearing, and motor skills. Click or tap Next after each set of questions. When you're done, Windows adjusts itself to what Microsoft believes are optimal settings for your abilities.

You can also click or tap the link to open the Ease of Use group, where you can access the Ease of Access control panel, including the Ease of Access Center. Click or tap the Ease of Access Center link to view a list of eight categories of settings you can visit in turn and adjust as you prefer.

The Ease of Access control panel also has a link for Speech Recognition. Click or tap it to set up Windows and a microphone so you can speak commands and dictate text to Windows, controlling it with your voice rather than your hands.

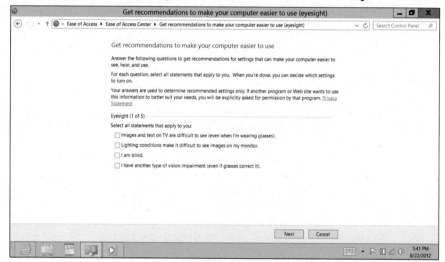

The quiz Microsoft provides to help determine optimal settings for your abilities

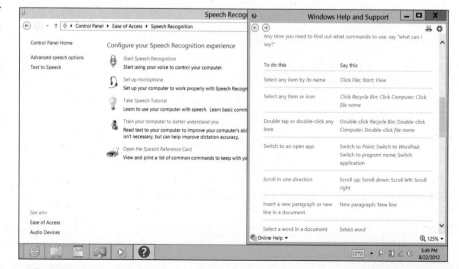

Enabling speech recognition

Connecting to Networks

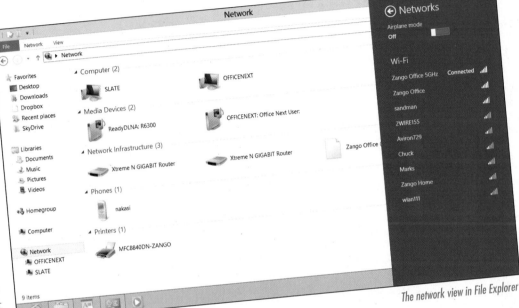

The network view in File Explorer

1 t's hard to find a home or an office with just one computer. These days, most people, even many kids, have their own PC. That means they need to share an Internet connection. And that means having a *network* in place to connect the PCs to the shared Internet device (usually a cable modem or DSL modem).

But such a network lets you do more than connect to the Internet from the same modem; you also can exchange files with each other and share devices such as printers. If you're a home entertainment geek, you can use the network to stream photos and movies to your HDTV if you own an Apple TV or similar device. And if you're a small business or even a geeky family, you might use the network to connect everyone to a shared hard disk for file repositories that everyone can access or back up to.

Networks may sound intimidating, but Windows 8 makes them easy. When your network is active, you can see what's connected to it in the Window Desktop's File Explorer by clicking or tapping Network in the Navigation pane.

Making the Connection

There are two kinds of networks you can use, and you often have both:

✔ **Ethernet network:** Devices are connected via cables to a central manager called a *router.*

✔ **Wi-Fi network:** Devices connect via radio waves to a router (or sometimes an access point, which has to be connected via Ethernet to a router).

These days, most routers provide both Ethernet and Wi-Fi; in fact, most cable modems and DSL modems come with built-in routers, so you can have just one box to plug into the wall. (If your cable or DSL modem has just one Ethernet port and no Wi-Fi, you connect a router to it via Ethernet, and everything else connects to that router.)

An Ethernet connection is faster than a Wi-Fi connection, but a Wi-Fi connection works anywhere you're in range of the signal. The range varies but is generally 40 to 200 feet based on the router's radio strength and the kinds of building materials in your home or office. (Concrete and metal can block or degrade Wi-Fi signals.)

Every router has its own setup instructions, so refer to those to get yours up and running. But chances are good that you already did that long ago for previously purchased PCs.

Connecting via Ethernet

Connecting a PC to a router via Ethernet is simple: Plug one end of the Ethernet cable into the Ethernet jack on the router and plug the other end to the Ethernet jack on the computer. If the router is properly set up and connected to the Internet, you'll get Internet access within seconds and have access to any other devices on your own network.

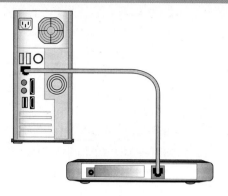

Connect your PC to an Ethernet network via a cable

Connecting wirelessly

Getting your PC connected via Wi-Fi is easier in Windows 8 than in previous versions. To connect to a nearby wireless network for the first time in Windows 8, follow these steps:

1 Open the Settings charm and check the status of the Network icon in the icon group at the bottom of the charm. If it shows a Wi-Fi network is available, click the Network icon.

2 Windows lists all the wireless networks within range of your PC. Connect to the desired Wi-Fi network by clicking or tapping its name.

3 Click the Connect button. (***Tip:*** If you check the adjacent Connect Automatically option before clicking or tapping the Connect button, Windows automatically connects to that network the next time you're within range, sparing you from connecting manually each time.)

4 If you're asked for a password, provide it. Then click Next.

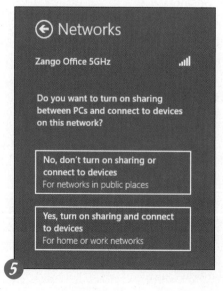

5 You're then asked whether you want to enable sharing between your PC and others on the network as well as connect to any devices (such as printers) detected. Click or tap the Yes or No button. (Click No when in a public place, such as a café hot spot, so others on this network can't spy on your PC's data.)

DUMMIES

You can also use cellular 3G and 4G networks to connect to the Internet, either using a built-in radio in a tablet or through a device called a MiFi. Cellular carriers offer such access typically through monthly subscription or pay-as-you-go plans, and they sell or rent any needed hardware. To turn on such cellular access, open the Settings charm, click or tap Change PC Settings, go to Wireless, and set the Mobile Broadband switch to On.

Getting to know the Networks icon

The Networks icon's appearance in the Settings charm varies based on your connection status. From left to right, here are the icons you may see:

 Wireless Available

 Wireless Unavailable

 Wired Connected

Wired Unavailable

WARNING!

Some Wi-Fi networks require that you enter a password to gain access. You should require a password on your own Wi-Fi network so strangers can't get in and hijack your Internet connection or, worse, access and perhaps cause harm to your PC and other network devices. You set up that password requirement in your router, not in Windows. We suggest you choose the WPA-2 level of security and that the password you require be short and memorable yet use mixed characters, such as **One+One=2**.

Managing the Connection

When your PC is connected to the desired network, there's rarely a need to disconnect. If you're using a wired Ethernet connection, just leave it plugged in all the time — unless of course when you need to move the PC to where the cable won't reach! To disconnect a wired connection, just unplug the Ethernet cable from your PC.

If you're using Wi-Fi, when your PC is out of signal range, you're automatically disconnected, but you'll automatically be reconnected when you're back in range if you selected the Connect Automatically option when first connecting. If you didn't select that option, you need to click and tap the desired Wi-Fi network again in the Settings charm when you're back in range.

Here's some additional info on managing Wi-Fi connections:

- **Connect to a different Wi-Fi network:** If you want to change Wi-Fi networks where several are available, just open the Settings charm, click or tap the Networks icon, and click the desired new Wi-Fi network from the list.

- **Disconnect from a Wi-Fi network:** If you want to disconnect from the current Wi-Fi network without switching to a different one, right-click or tap and hold the connected network's name and click or tap the Disconnect button that appears.

- **Disable all wireless connections — Wi-Fi, Bluetooth, and (if you have it) cellular:** The easiest way to disable all connections is to set

Disconnecting from a Wi-Fi network

the Airplane Mode switch to On in the Settings charm's Networks list. You use this mode when on an airplane so as not to interfere with the plane's electronics during takeoff and landing. It's also a great way to save on battery usage for a laptop or tablet at times when you don't need any of these services active.

Show estimated data usage

Set as metered connection

Forget this network

Turn sharing on or off

View connection properties

Disconnect

Zango Office

Chuck

2WIRE155

The menu of options for a Wi-Fi network

services often have caps on how much data you can use. The amount of usage appears beneath the network's name, as well as the Reset link, which you can use to set the usage figure back to zero, such as when beginning a new month's data plan.

✔ **Set as Metered Connection:** Use this option to tell Windows the wireless connection is metered — that is, capped or paid by the amount you use, such as for a cellular connection. That way, Windows won't use this connection in some circumstances. (For example, from the PC Settings screen's Sync Your Settings pane, you can disable syncing of settings for metered connections. Also, you can disable syncing for Store, Music, and Video downloads in their respective Settings charms.) You can change the connection back to an unmetered one by choosing Set as Non-Metered Connection in the menu.

✔ **Forget This Network:** Click or tap this option to stop Windows from auto-connecting to the network when in range.

✔ **Turn Sharing On or Off:** This option opens a pane where you can enable or disable sharing of files, printers, and other resources with other devices on the network.

✔ **View Connection Properties:** Click or tap this option to open a dialog box on the Windows Desktop, where you can apply advanced settings to this connection.

More controls are available for your network connections. To see them, right-click or tap and hold a network's name in the Settings charm (note that not all options appear for all types of network connections):

✔ **Show Estimated Data Usage:** Click or tap this option to see how much traffic you've sent and received over this connection. It's meant for PC tablets that have cellular radios, whose

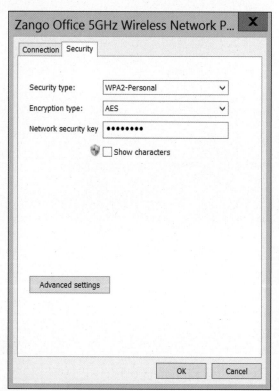

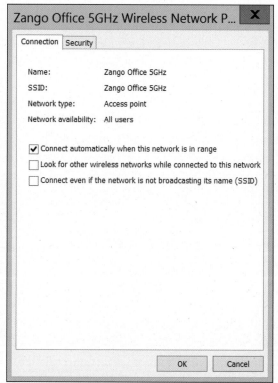

The two panes of the settings dialog box for a network connection

Working with Homegroups

● *Homegroups explained* ● *Enabling and managing file sharing*
● *Making your printer available to others*

Creating a network between your computers makes it easier for them to share resources: an Internet connection, printers, and even your files. But how can you share some files while keeping others private?

Microsoft's solution is called a *homegroup*. A simpler way of networking, a homegroup lets every Windows PC in the house share the files nearly everybody wants to share: music, photos, movies, and the household printer.

Homegroups aren't limited to Windows 8 computers, either — they work fine with any Windows 7 computers on your network, as well. (Homegroups *don't* work with Windows Vista or XP, unfortunately.)

Creating a Homegroup

Here's how to set up a new homegroup on a Windows 8 PC, as well as how to let Windows 8 join a homegroup you may have already set up with your other networked computers:

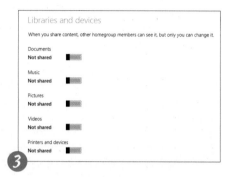

1 Open the Settings charm and click or tap Change PC Settings to open PC Settings.

2 Click or tap the Homegroup category on the left to open the Homegroup pane. Then click or tap either the Create or Join button. (The button you see depends on whether a homegroup has already been set up and is detected by Windows 8.)

3 If you click or tap the Create button, a pane of options for what you can share appears. Note that the Documents, Music, Pictures, and Videos options refer to files stored in your My Documents, My Music, My Pictures, and My Videos folders, respectively. Scroll down to see the password others need to use to access the shared items. (If your option was Join and you clicked or tapped it, you'll be asked to enter the password set by whoever created the homegroup.)

Don't know the homegroup's password? You can find it in the Windows Desktop's File Explorer by right-clicking or tapping and holding the Homegroup option in the Navigation pane and choosing View the Homegroup Password from the menu that appears.

Homegroups are handy if you don't want to share with others. If you have multiple computers — say, a laptop and a PC tablet — you could use a homegroup and shared folders to move or copy files easily between them.

DUMMIES

Managing Access to Shared Files

When you create or join a homegroup, you can choose what libraries to share only from your *own* account. If other account holders on that same PC also want to share their libraries, they should do this: In File Explorer, right-click or tap and hold Homegroup in the Navigation pane and then choose Change Homegroup Settings to open a dialog box of sharable items. There, they need to add check marks to the items they want to share and then click or tap Save Changes.

When you share libraries on homegroups, you want your friends and family to marvel over your photos of Costa Rican tree frogs, for example, but you don't want anybody to delete or otherwise mess up your original files. The good folks at Microsoft know that, so by default, any files in your shared files are *read-only* — they can't be deleted or have any changes saved to that folder. (People can work on copies stored on their own PCs.)

If you do want people to be able to delete and change shared files, you need to put the files in a public folder. But where are the public folders? You don't see them in My Documents, My Pictures, and so on in File Explorer. They're there, but they're concealed in the Navigation pane. Click or tap a folder in the Libraries section to reveal its subfolders. If you've enabled sharing for that folder, you see two folders lists, such as My Music and Public Music. Simply drag files into Public Music (or whatever public folder is appropriate) so other people on the network or with accounts on your PC can work on the files directly. They too will need to go to the public folder via File Explorer's Navigation pane to see the contents.

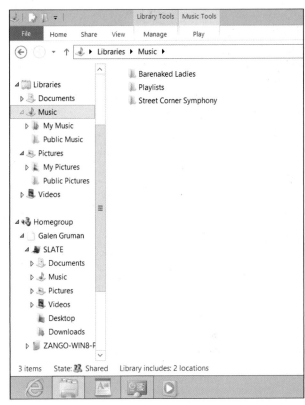

The Navigation pane is where you expose the public folders where others can edit and delete files, not just view them

---

Sharing between PCs and Macs

These days, Apple Macintoshes and Windows PCs are increasingly sharing quarters. So how do you share files between them over the network? On a Mac, you first need to enable file sharing for Windows by following these steps:

1. Go to the Sharing system preference application (choose ➡ System Preferences and then click the Sharing icon) and select File Sharing.

2. Click Options to open a settings sheet where you select the Share Files and Folders Using SMB (Windows) option. Select the accounts whose files you want to share and then click Done.

3. Add folders to the Shared Folders list by clicking the + icon. Be sure to set permissions to Read & Write, Read Only, or Write Only (Dropbox) as appropriate for each shared folder.

4. Take note the name of the Mac in the pane, ignoring the **.local** part, and then close the system preference window.

With Windows file sharing enabled on the Mac, open File Explorer on your PC and enter ***Mac name*** in the text field at the top of the window, to the right of the Network label. The Mac's shared folders become visible and now work just like any other folders in Windows.

The Mac won't show up in the standard view of connected items you see when you click or tap Network in File Explorer's Navigation pane, but you can return to it easily at anytime by clicking or tapping the unnamed menu between the → icon and ↑ icon at the top of File Explorer, beneath the menus, and then choosing its name from the list that appears.

Accessing What Others Have Shared

To see the shared libraries of other people on your PC and network, open File Explorer on the Windows Desktop and click or tap the Homegroup option in the Navigation pane. File Explorer's right pane promptly lists the names and icons of every person (whether on your PC or on the network) who has chosen to share files on an existing homegroup. Click the Join Now button below that list and enter that account's homegroup password to gain access to the shared files and resources.

After you've joined the homegroup, you can browse each person's shared folders simply by double-clicking or double-tapping that person's name in the homegroup window.

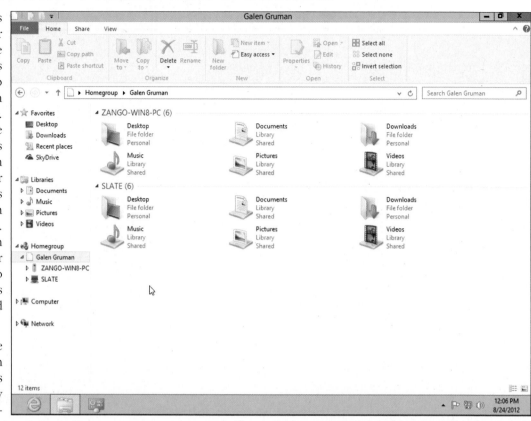

Browsing shared homegroups in File Manager

You can do more than browse those folders:

- **Opening:** To open a file on a shared library, double-click or double-tap its icon, just as you would any other file. The appropriate program opens it. If you see an error message, the file uses an app you don't own. Your solution? Buy or download the program from the Internet or ask the person to save the file in a format that one of your apps can open.

- **Copying:** To copy a file from another person's homegroup, drag it into your own library. Alternatively, select the file and press Ctrl+C to copy it; then go into the folder where you want to put the copied file and press Ctrl+V to paste it.

- **Deleting or changing:** You can delete or change some, but not all, of the items in another person's homegroup.

Sharing a Printer on the Network

If you've turned on the homegroups, Windows makes sharing a printer extraordinarily easy. After you plug a USB printer into a Windows 8 PC, you're set: Windows automatically recognizes the newly plugged-in printer as soon as it's turned on, and it tells other networked PCs about it, too, whether the PCs are running Windows 8, Windows 7, Windows Vista, or Windows XP. The shared printer automatically appears in apps' Print dialog boxes and menus, in both the Windows Desktop and Start screen.

Windows allows you to join only one homegroup at a time, so in effect you're limited to one homegroup on any one network, such as at your home. Essentially, the first PC to create a homegroup becomes the homegroup used by all other PCs that choose to join in.

Setting Up Safety Controls

● *Using Windows Defender* ● *Configuring Internet Explorer's defenses*
● *Safeguarding your privacy* ● *The pros and cons of permissions*
● *Using the Action Center*

1 f you've used a PC for any length of time, you know that the web and e-mail are wondrous technologies, making research, commerce, and communications amazingly rich and easy. But you also know that there's big danger out in the wilds of the Internet, from scammers pretending you have unknown riches coming your way to Trojan, virus, spyware, and worm apps — known collectively as *malware* — that steal your bank account information, trash your files, or worse.

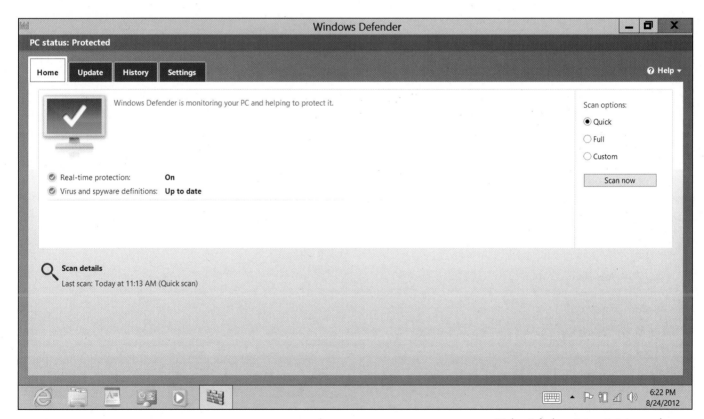

Windows Defender protects against viruses and spyware

Taking these basic steps can help you avoid falling for these scams and inviting malware in:

- **Don't open e-mails from people you don't know and companies you don't do business with.** Immediately delete them instead.

- **Be suspicious of any e-mails from people you do know and companies you do business with that ask for information or to click embedded web links.** (This technique is called *phishing.*) Most are fake, and some are very convincing fakes. Send a new e-mail to your friends (don't reply to the suspect messages) asking whether they really sent the messages. And go directly to the company websites (don't go there via a link embedded in the e-mail, though) and log in to your accounts to see whether there really is updated information needed. Otherwise, you may unwittingly allow malware to be downloaded to your PC or give thieves the keys to your accounts.

- **Don't download "free" apps, music, or videos from file-sharing sites.** Almost all are filled with malware. Even just going to those sites can infect your PC. Only go to legitimate sites — and go there yourself, not from an e-mail link.

Given that about three-quarters of all e-mail is *spam* — those unsolicited come-ons, mostly from scammers — it's easy to mistakenly click an evil web link or open one whose embedded photo hides malware. That's where technology can help, and Windows has plenty of it. Just be clear: The technology is not perfect, so your first line of defense is to be cautious and suspicious, not to rely on the technology to protect you from the evil once you open the door.

Requiring Passwords

Every PC — and every account on a PC — should be secured with a password. Using a Microsoft account requires use of a password, and for local accounts, Windows 8 encourages you to use a password when you set up the accounts.

If you haven't yet set a password, do so in the Users pane of the PC Settings screen (accessible from the Settings charm).

Avoiding Viruses with Windows Defender

When it comes to viruses, *everything* is suspect. Viruses travel not only through e-mail messages, programs, files, networks, and USB thumb drives, but also in screen savers, themes, toolbars, and other Windows add-ons.

To combat the problem, Windows 8 includes a new version of Windows Defender that incorporates Microsoft Security Essentials, a security and antivirus program Microsoft has long offered as a free download.

Windows Defender scans everything that enters your computer, whether through downloads, e-mail, networks, messaging programs, or external drives. If Windows Defender notices something evil trying to enter your computer, it lets you know with a message wherever you are, in the Windows Desktop or Start screen environment. Then Windows Defender quarantines the virus, rendering it unable to infect your computer.

All the security apps and settings for Windows 8 reside on the Windows Desktop, not on the Start screen.

Windows Defender constantly scans your PC in the background. But if your PC acts strange or you'd just feel better to check yourself, tell Windows Defender to scan your PC immediately. Here's how to open Windows Defender:

- The easiest way is to go to the Start screen and type **Windows Defender** and then click or tap its name in the results list that appears.

- If you don't have a physical keyboard, open the Start screen's App bar, click or tap All Apps, and then scroll until you find the Windows Defender tile and click it.

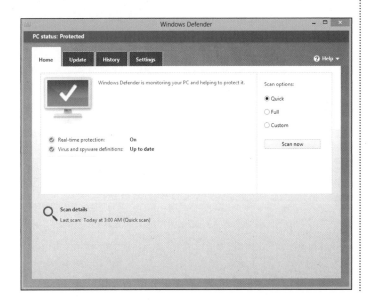

In the main Windows Defender window, click or tap the Scan Now button. If you think you have something nasty lurking deep in your PC, before you click or tap Scan Now, select the Full option from the scan options that appear above the Scan Now button.

Windows Defender normally doesn't scan flash drives and portable hard drives. To include them, go to its Settings pane (click or tap the Settings tab to switch to it), select Advanced from the list at left, and then select the Scan Removable Drives check box. Click or tap Save Changes to save the changes.

Don't run more than one antivirus app, because they often quarrel. If you want to test a different program, first disable Windows Defender by going to its Settings pane, selecting the Administrator option, and then deselecting the Turn On Windows Defender check box. Restart your PC and then install the new antivirus app. If you decide not to use the new one, uninstall it and re-enable Windows Defender by selecting the Turn On Windows Defender check box.

Staying Safe on the Internet

The Internet is not a safe place. Some people design websites specifically to exploit the latest vulnerabilities in Windows — the ones Microsoft hasn't yet patched. But you can reduce your risk by using the security settings in Internet Explorer (IE) 10.

Reducing the success of phishing scams

When you first run Internet Explorer, make sure its SmartScreen filter is turned on by clicking or tapping the Tools icon (shown in the margin) and choosing Safety from the top menu. When the Safety menu appears, choose Turn On SmartScreen Filter if you see it (because that means it was turned off). If you see Turn Off SmartScreen Filter, leave it be — you're already protected.

What SmartScreen does is compares a website's address with a list of known phishing sites. If it finds a match, the SmartScreen filter warns you against opening the web page. Heed its advice.

You can warn Microsoft if you spot a site that smells suspiciously like phish. Choose Tools→Safety→Report Unsafe Website from Internet Explorer's menu bar. Internet Explorer takes you to Microsoft's SmartScreen Filter website to report the evildoer so Microsoft can investigate and warn other users if it finds the site is for phishing.

You change the security settings in the Windows Desktop version of IE 10, and your settings apply to the Start screen version as well.

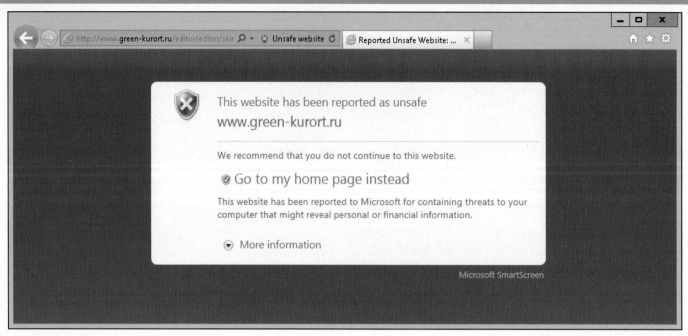

If enabled, IE 10's SmartScreen warns you of suspected phishing sites

Setting security zones

IE 10 uses a technology called *security zones* that determines the level of protection to apply to websites you visit. The default settings work well and should be changed only for good reason. To see or change the settings, choose Tools➔Internet Options and then go to the Security pane in the Internet Options dialog box that opens.

IE 10 offers four security zones, each offering a different level of protection. When you add different websites to different zones, IE 10 treats those sites differently, placing restrictions on some and lifting restrictions for others. Here's the rundown:

- **Internet:** IE 10 treats *every* website as if it were in this catch-all zone. This zone comes preset to offer Internet Explorer's medium-high security level, which works very well for most needs.

- **Local Intranet:** This zone is intended for websites running on an *internal* network. (Home users rarely have to deal with intranets because they're mostly found in corporations.) Because internal websites are created in-house and are self-contained, this zone removes some security restrictions, letting you do more things.

- **Trusted Sites:** Putting sites in here means you trust them *completely* (such as your bank's website).

- **Restricted Sites:** If you don't trust a site at all but still need to visit it, place that shady site's web address in here. IE 10 then lets you visit the site but not download from it or use any of its *plug-ins* — small downloadable programs adding extra graphics, animation, and similar enhancements.

If you fiddled with the security settings and suspect you've changed them for the worse, you're not stuck. Just click the Reset All Zones to Default Level button in the Internet Options dialog box's Security pane.

Avoiding evil add-ons

Microsoft designed Internet Explorer to let programmers add extra features through *add-ons* (also called *plug-ins*). By installing an add-on program — toolbars, stock tickers, and program launchers, for example — you can wring a little more work out of IE 10.

Unfortunately, dastardly programmers began creating add-ons that *harm* users. Some add-ons spy on your activities, bombard your screen with ads, or redirect your home page to another site. Worst yet, some renegade add-ons install themselves as soon as you visit a website — without asking your permission.

Windows 8 packs several guns to combat these troublemakers. First, if a site tries to sneak a program onto your computer, IE 10 quickly blocks it. Then IE 10 places a warning message across the bottom of its window. Clicking or tapping the Install button installs the program. Then click or tap the Enable button to turn on your new IE 10 add-on.

TIP

Can't find the unwanted add-on? Use the Show menu to switch among seeing All Add-Ons, Currently Loaded Add-Ons, Run Without Permission, and Downloaded Controls. Then select the errant add-on and click Disable.

Unfortunately, IE 10 can't tell the good downloads from the bad, leaving the burden of proof to you. So, if you see an installation alert and you *haven't* requested a download, chances are good that the site is trying to harm you: Don't click the Install button. Instead, click one of your Favorite links or your Home icon to quickly move to a new website.

If a bad add-on creeps in somehow, you're not completely out of luck. Internet Explorer's Add-On Manager lets you disable it. To see all the add-on programs installed in Internet Explorer (and remove any that you know are bad, unnecessary, or just plain bothersome), choose Tools➜Manage Add-Ons, and in the Manage Add-Ons dialog box that appears, select the errant add-on and click or tap the Disable button.

Blocking intruders with a firewall

Windows uses a technology called a *firewall* that blocks outsiders from getting into your PC via your Internet connection. It should always be turned on — no exceptions. Windows 8 turns it on by default, but if it gets turned off either accidentally or by malware, turn it back on by using the Action Center, described later in this article.

Controlling Your Privacy

As you get more and more connected and use more and more online services with accounts, other people — mainly companies — can track a lot of information about you. That can make the services work better by being more personalized and contextual, but it also allows for exposing your personal habits, preferences, and activities to strangers who might use it against you, such as to limit your health insurance, deny you a job, or embarrass you publicly.

When you sign up for a service online, your activities on that service are tracked. When you visit a website — especially a commercial one — your activities are tracked.

This website wants to install the following add-on: 'Smiley Central Add-ons' from 'Mindspark Interactive Network'. What's the risk?

IE 10 alerts you about installing add-ons just in case a bad one is trying to sneak into your PC

For the first time, Windows can now track your location, too, if you let it. So, for example, any photo you take includes data on where you were when you took it.

But there are steps you can take to protect your privacy, revealing only what you must for a service worth the price in privacy:

✔ **When an app wants access to your location information, the first time you use it, it asks for permission; click or tap Block if there's not a good-enough reason to share your location with that app.** To later deny location-tracking permission for an app you granted permission to, open its Settings charm, click or tap Permissions, and set its Location switch to Off. You can turn off all location tracking in the Privacy pane of the PC Settings screen (accessible via the Settings charm) by setting the Let Apps Use My Location switch to Off.

✔ **Review the permissions for each of your apps.** To review permissions, open the app's Settings charm, click or tap Permissions, and see what's listed in the Privacy section. You can turn off some of these permissions such as location tracking and search-history retention for that app right there.

✔ **Get a separate e-mail address that you use just for your Microsoft account.** That way only your activities on your PC, at the Windows Store, and at SkyDrive are trackable by Microsoft. Likewise, get a separate e-mail address you use for other services such as Facebook and Amazon.com, so no one can track all your activities across all your services because they are tied to a single e-mail account. (This also helps if someone steals your account information, because it limits what else they can access.)

✔ **Don't use Google's Gmail or Microsoft's Hotmail or Outlook.com.** Google scans every e-mail sent or received so it can match ads to what you're interested in. Who knows what else it does with that data? Microsoft swears it doesn't use the personal data, but why take the risk? An e-mail client such as Outlook or Thunderbird doesn't track you.

✔ **In browsers, always use "private" browsing so your web visits aren't tracked.** In Internet Explorer, it's called *InPrivate;* Firefox calls it *Incognito;* Chrome uses *Private Browsing*. InPrivate browsing is available only in the Windows Desktop version of IE 10; choose Tools➔Safety➔InPrivate Browsing or press Ctrl+Shift+P to enable it.

Those Annoying Permission Requests

After more than 20 years of development, Windows is still pretty naïve. Sometimes when you run a program or try to change a setting on your PC, Windows can't tell whether *you're* doing the work or *malware* is trying to move in.

The Windows solution? When Windows 8 notices anybody (or anything) trying to change something that can potentially harm Windows or your PC, it darkens the screen and flashes a message asking for permission.

If one of these permission messages appears unexpectedly, Windows 8 may be warning you about a bit of nastiness trying to sneak in. So click No or Don't Install to deny it permission. But if *you're* trying to do something specific with your PC and Windows 8 puts up its boxing gloves, click Yes or Install, instead. Windows 8 drops its guard and lets you in.

Click Don't Install if a permissions message like this appears out of the blue.

But, wait, there's more: If your account doesn't have administrator privileges, you can't simply approve the deed. You must track down someone with administrator privileges and ask him or her to type in the administrator password. The good news about this extra work is that it's also an extra challenge for the people who write the malware.

If you have an administrator password, you can restrain Windows 8 from asking for confirmation, though doing so means there's more risk of something unwanted sneaking in. So don't do it unless you are a vigilant, safe-computing kind of person.

To make Windows stop asking for confirmation, open Control Panel, click or tap the User Accounts and Family Safety link, and click the User Accounts icon. The Make Changes to your User Account page appears. Click or tap the Change User Account Control Settings link. A slider appears onscreen, set three-quarters of the way up to Default. To reduce the permissions intrusions, move the slider down; to increase its strictness, slide it up. Click or tap OK after choosing your comfort level.

Managing Your Safety in the Action Center

 Take a minute to check your PC's safety with the Windows Desktop's Action Center. Part of Control Panel, the Action Center displays any problems it notices with the Windows 8 main defenses, and it provides handy, one-button fixes for the situations. Its taskbar icon, the white flag shown in the margin, always shows the Action Center's current status.

The Action Center window color-codes problems by their severity; a blood red band shows critical problems requiring immediate action, and a yellow band means the problem needs attention soon.

If any of your computer's security defenses aren't loaded and pointing in the right direction, the Action Center's taskbar icon appears with a red X across the flag. When you spot that red-flagged icon on your taskbar, click or tap the Action Center icon and choose Open Action Center from the menu that appears. After the Action Center opens, click or tap the button next to flagged items to fix the potential security problems.

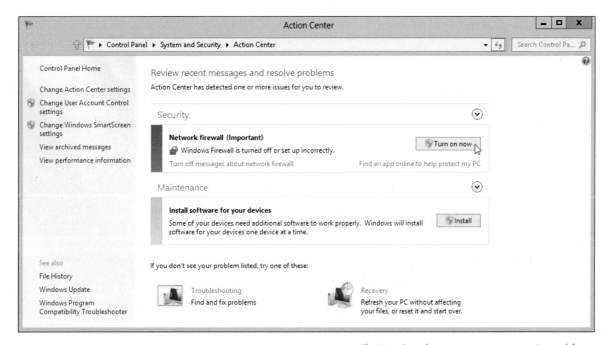

The Action Center lets you turn on your computer's main defenses.

Backing Up with File History

● *Setting up backups* ● *Restoring files and data to your PC*

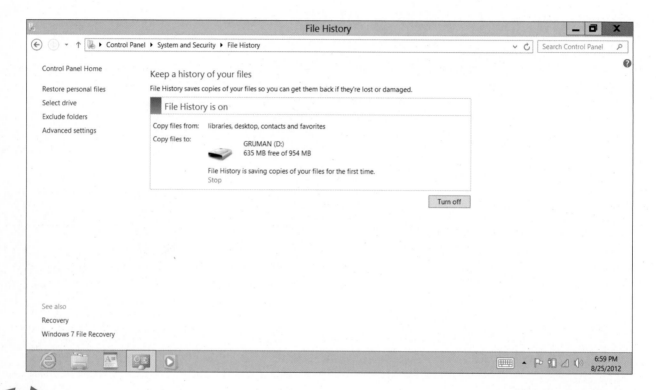

Your hard drive will eventually die, unfortunately, and it will take everything down with it: years of digital photos, music, letters, financial records, scanned memorabilia, and anything else you've created or stored on your PC.

That's why you must back up your files on a regular basis. When your hard drive finally walks off the stage, your backup copy lets you keep the show on the road.

Windows 8 includes a new backup solution called *File History*. After you turn it on, File History automatically backs up every file in your libraries — where the My Pictures, My Videos, My Documents, and My Music folders reside — every hour. The program is easy to turn on, is simple to figure out, runs automatically, and backs up everything you need.

But before File History can go to work, you need an external hard drive to hold the backups. These drives are inexpensive and plug in easily via a USB port. Many don't need their own power supply, though these models cost more. Be sure to get an external drive with at least twice the capacity of your computer's internal hard drive to give you room to store multiple versions of your files, so you can go back to specific versions when needed.

File History saves your *own* data, not your apps or Windows itself. After all, apps and Windows can always be reinstalled from their installation discs, installer downloads (which you might want to copy to a recordable CD for safety), or the Windows Store.

Setting Up File History

Follow these steps to tell your PC to start backing up your work automatically every hour:

Removable Disk (K:)

Choose what to do with removable drives.

Speed up my system
Windows ReadyBoost

Configure this drive for backup
File History

Open folder to view files
Windows Explorer

Take no action

1 Plug your drive into your PC via its USB cable and make sure it's turned on.

Removable Disk (K:)
Tap to choose what happens with removable drives.

2 Click or tap the pop-up notification that says, "Tap to choose what happens with removable drives." This notification appears when you connect any new storage device.

3 Select the Configure This Drive for Backup option.

File History

System and Security ▸ File History

Keep a history of your files

File History saves copies of your files so you can get them back if they're lost or damaged.

File History is off

Copy files from: libraries, desktop, contacts and favorites
Copy files to:
                   16GB SDHC (H:)
                   9.99 GB free of 14.9 GB

☐ I want to use a previous backup on this File History drive.   Turn on

4 When the File History window appears, click or tap the Turn On button. File History begins saving copies of your files, which may take several hours the first time.

TIP

When connecting a new hard drive, you may see a pop-up asking whether you'd like to recommend this drive to other members of your homegroup. If it's a large drive meant for everybody on your computer to share, click or tap Yes. If you'd like to keep it for your personal backups, click or tap No.

You can also set up File History in the Control Panel, as well as change the drive used for backup there. To do so, click or tap the System and Security link and then click or tap the File History link. The File History app opens and takes a guess as to which drive you want to begin filling with your backups. If you need to use a different drive, click or tap the Select Drive link in the window's left pane and select the desired drive. Then click or tap the Turn On button.

Although File History does a remarkable job at keeping everything easy to use and automatic, it comes with a few bits of fine print, described here:

- ✔ If you try to save to a shared drive on another PC, Windows 8 asks you to enter a username and password from an administrator account on the other PC.

- ✔ File History backs up everything in your libraries, Documents, Music, Pictures, and Videos, as well as what's in the Public folders. That's natural because that's where you store your files. To exclude some folders in those libraries (perhaps exclude your Videos folder if you already have copies of your videos), click or tap the Exclude Folders option in the File History window's left pane.

- ✔ Windows 8 normally backs up files automatically every hour. To change that schedule, click or tap the Advanced Settings option in the File History window's left pane. Then choose the backup frequency, which ranges from every 10 minutes to once a day.

Recovering Data from File History

File History lets you restore backups from any of your libraries, desktop, contacts, or Internet Explorer favorites

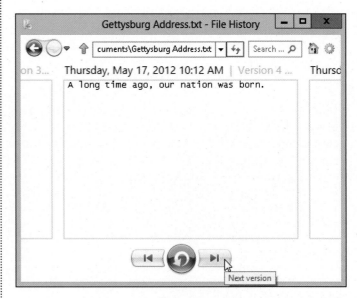

Use the arrow buttons in File History to navigate among versions of a file.

History   To browse through your backed up files and folders, restoring the ones you want, open the folder containing the items you'd like to retrieve. If you want to restore a previous version of a particular file, be sure to select that file. On the Ribbon's Home tab (click or tap Home to see it), click or tap the History button, shown in the margin.

Clicking the History button opens the File History app, which looks much like a plain old folder. It shows what's been backed up: your libraries, your desktop, your contacts, and your favorite websites.

Open the folders to find what you want to restore. After you've found what you want, here's how to select what you want to restore:

- **All libraries:** To restore all libraries — such as after refreshing your PC — select Libraries in the File History window.

- **Library:** To restore an entire library — perhaps your Documents library — select the Documents library in the File History window. (Don't open the Documents library; just click or tap it once to select it.)

- **Folder:** To restore an entire folder, open the library where it resides. When you can see the folder, select it — again, don't open it.

- **Files:** To restore a group of files, open the folder containing them so the files' icons are onscreen.

- **One file:** To restore an earlier version of a file, open that file from inside the File History window; File History displays that file's contents.

As you decide what to restore, you can browse through different versions of what you're currently viewing, by using the ← and → icons at the bottom of the screen to move backward and forward in time, respectively, through your backed-up copies. As you move forward and backward through the versions, feel free to open libraries, folders, or individual files, peeking inside them until you're looking at the version that you want to retrieve.

When you've selected what you want to restore, click or tap the Restore button (the curved-arrow icon). File History puts the selected files and folders back in its original location. If a newer version of a selected item is in that same location,

a dialog box appears, asking how you want to resolve the conflicting versions. You can replace the current file with the one you chose to restore, you can skip the restore and leave the current file in place, or you can keep both files in the original location. (The restored file gets a numeral appended to its name in that case.)

When you're done restoring, exit File History by closing its window.

DUMMIES

Setting Up Parental Controls

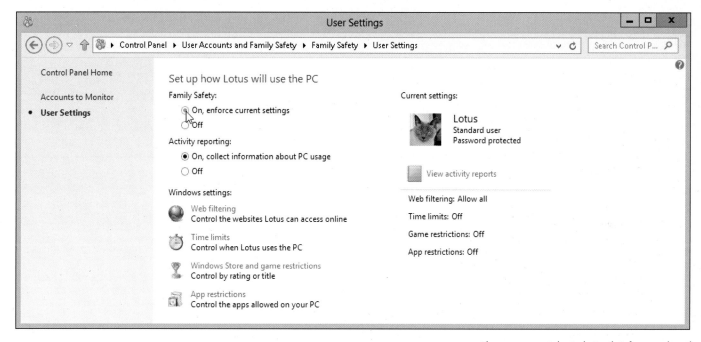

	User Settings	_ □ X

◀ ◉ ▽ ⬆ ⬢ ▸ Control Panel ▸ User Accounts and Family Safety ▸ Family Safety ▸ User Settings ⌄ ↻   Search Control P... 🔍

Control Panel Home

Accounts to Monitor

● **User Settings**

Set up how Lotus will use the PC

Family Safety:
◉ On, enforce current settings
○ Off

Activity reporting:
◉ On, collect information about PC usage
○ Off

Windows settings:

🌐 Web filtering
Control the websites Lotus can access online

⏱ Time limits
Control when Lotus uses the PC

🏆 Windows Store and game restrictions
Control by rating or title

📋 App restrictions
Control the apps allowed on your PC

Current settings:

Lotus
Standard user
Password protected

View activity reports

Web filtering: Allow all

Time limits: Off

Game restrictions: Off

App restrictions: Off

The user account window in the Family Safety control panel

A feature much-welcomed by parents and much-booed by their children, the Family Safety control panel offers several ways to police how people can access the computer, as well as the Internet. People who share their PC with roommates should use Family Safety as well.

Family Safety works best under these conditions:

- The PC's owner or manager must have an administrator account. Everyone else — especially children or your roommates — should have standard accounts so they can't override your Family Safety settings.

- If your children have their own PCs, create an administrator account on their PCs for yourself. Then change their accounts to standard so they can't override your Family Safety settings.

TIP

Although the Family Safety controls work well, few things in the computer world are foolproof. If you're worried about your children's computer usage, check up on them in person, and maybe check their browsing history and e-mail and messaging accounts periodically as well.

Safety and Security

To set up Family Safety, take these steps:

1 Open the Control Panel, and in the User Accounts and Family Safety section, click or tap Set Up Family Safety for Any User.

2 Click or tap the icon or name of the user to whom you want to apply Family Settings. (If that person has administrator privileges, you'll be asked whether to change the person's account type to standard, which you must do if you want to apply Family Safety settings to that account.)

3 Select the On, Enforce Current Settings option and then go through the various settings described next and set them as desired.

Here are the types of Family Safety settings you can impose:

- **Web Filtering:** To supervise small children, click or tap this link. In the window that appears, select the *Name* Can Use Only the Websites I Allow option. Use the Set Web Filtering Level link to choose from five levels of filtering and to optionally disable file downloads. Use the Allow or Block Specific Websites link to enter the web addresses for websites you want to allow or block — you can do both in the window that appears.

- **Time Limits:** This link opens a window from which you can set how many hours the user can use the PC each day, as well as what time period the user can use the PC — a curfew, basically. The curfew can be set separately for each day of the week.

- **Windows Store and Game Restrictions:** You may allow or ban *all* games here, restrict access to games with certain ratings (ratings appear on most software boxes), and block or allow individual games.

- **App Restrictions:** You can block all apps (both Windows Desktop and Start screen apps), or you can allow access to only a handful of programs by selecting their check boxes in the list of installed apps.

Be sure to click or tap the View All Reports link in each user's Family Safety control panel to see what activity Windows has recorded them doing.

FOR DUMMIES

Refreshing and Restoring Windows

PC settings

Personalize

Users

Notifications

Search

Share

General

Privacy

Devices

Ease of Access

Sync your settings

HomeGroup

Windows Update

Language

Add or change input methods, keyboard layouts, and languages.
Language preferences

Available storage

You have 24.0 GB available. See how much space your apps are using.

View app sizes

Refresh your PC without affecting your files

To use this feature, sign in as an administrator.

Remove everything and reinstall Windows

To use this feature, sign in as an administrator.

Advanced startup

Start up from a device or disc (such as a USB drive or DVD), change Windows startup settings, or restore Windows from a system image. This will restart your PC. All users will be signed out and could lose any unsaved work.

Restart now

Glitch happens. The computer misbehaves, a program crashes, or the machine becomes unexpectedly slow. If your computer is misbehaving, try refreshing it, which sets Windows back to its original condition, removes any Windows Desktop apps you installed (Start screen apps are retained), but leaves any files in the libraries — where your photos, music, videos, and documents reside — unmolested. If refreshing doesn't work, you can reset your PC, which essentially erases everything and makes you start all over again from scratch (which is why you should use File History to restore your data in such a situation).

You should also create a recovery disk so you can start your PC should something go wrong on its hard drive. You'll need a recordable CD, recordable DVD, USB thumb drive, or USB hard drive — it doesn't matter which — to contain the recovery files and act as the recovery disk if needed. To do so, open Control Panel and enter **recover** in its search box and then press Enter or click or tap the Search button (the magnifying-glass icon). Click or tap the Recovery icon that appears and, in the Recovery control panel that opens, click the Create Recovery Drive link and follow the instructions.

Refreshing a PC

Windows 8 makes it very easy to refresh your PC: Open PC Settings in the Settings charm, go to the General pane, and scroll down to the bottom. Under the heading Refresh Your PC without Affecting Your Files, click or tap the Get Started button. A screen appears letting you know what will be removed. Click or tap Next to continue.

Windows may need your original Windows 8 installation disc or a recovery disk before proceeding. If so, it will ask you to insert either one. If you don't have the required media, click or tap Cancel — you can't refresh your PC.

Click or tap the Refresh button to begin the refresh process, your PC will restart at least once. When the refresh process is complete, the Lock screen appears. Sign in as usual. Go to the Windows Desktop and look for a file named *Removed Apps* on the desktop; double-click or double-tap it to open the file in Internet Explorer so you can see a list of Windows Desktop apps that were removed. If you're aware that one of these apps created a problem or don't recognize an app (that's a sign it could be malware), don't reinstall it.

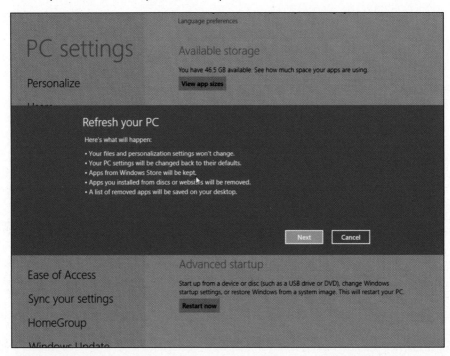

Keeping Windows up-to-date

Things change. Microsoft enhances some Windows capabilities, it adds support for new hardware devices, it fixes some bugs in its software, and it finds new malware for Windows Defender to block. To get those updates to you, Microsoft includes the Windows Update feature in Windows 8. The updates are automatically downloaded and installed for you, as long as your PC has an Internet connection.

But if you want to force an update — maybe you read about a new update and your PC hasn't yet gotten around to installing it — you can force it by going to the PC Settings screen and accessing the Windows Update pane.

If there are any updates downloaded but not yet installed, you'll see a note to that effect, as well as a link you can click or tap to force the installation immediately. You can also check for updates not yet downloaded by clicking or tapping the Check for Updates Now button.

It really is that easy.

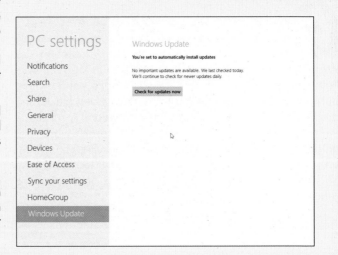

For DUMMIES

Wiping Your PC for a Clean Start

The refresh function is the best choice for handling a Windows PC that may have corrupted Windows or application files, or where malware is lurking that Windows Defender can't root out. Sometimes, though, you need to truly wipe out the PC. Perhaps you're giving your old PC to someone else and want to make sure no personal information is left on it. Perhaps something has gone so terribly wrong in Windows that the only way to fix it is to essentially start over. That's what the reset function is for.

Before you reset your computer, make sure you have a complete backup of all your files (you can use the File History feature) and all your installation discs or installation files (saved to an external drive or recordable disc). You don't need to save your Start screen apps because the Windows Store keeps a record of what you've downloaded and will re-download them for you on the new PC.

To wipe the PC, follow these steps:

1 Open the Settings charm and click the PC Settings link. Scroll down to the bottom of the General pane, and under the heading Remove Everything and Reinstall Windows, click or tap the Get Started button.

2 A screen appears, reminding you of what will be wiped out. Click or tap Next to continue. As with a PC refresh, you may need your original Windows installation disc or a recovery disk to continue.

3 One more screen appears, asking how you want to handle the removal of your personal files. You have two options. Select the *Thoroughly, but This Can Take Several Hours* option if you plan to sell the computer or give it to someone you don't know or trust. Select *Quickly, but Your Files Might Be Recoverable by Someone Else* if you're keeping the computer or giving it to someone you know and trust. Your files aren't likely to be recovered by most users other than computer ninjas (such as some 15-year-olds or computer science majors). Click or tap Reset to wipe your PC; your computer will restart at least once.

REMEMBER

When the Reset process is complete, your computer will be in pristine condition, with just Windows 8 installed. You need to set up your user accounts, reinstall your apps, and restore your files — just as if it were a brand-new PC.

Exploring Windows® 8 For Dummies®

Published by
John Wiley & Sons, Inc.
111 River Street
Hoboken, NJ 07030-5774

www.wiley.com

For general information on our other products and services, please contact our Customer Care Department within the U.S. at 877-762-2974, outside the U.S. at 317-572-3993, or fax 317-572-4002.

For technical support, please visit www.wiley.com/techsupport.

Wiley publishes in a variety of print and electronic formats and by print-on-demand. Some material included with standard print versions of this book may not be included in e-books or in print-on-demand. If this book refers to media such as a CD or DVD that is not included in the version you purchased, you may download this material at http://booksupport.wiley.com. For more information about Wiley products, visit www.wiley.com.

Library of Congress Control Number: 2012949798

ISBN 978-1-118-48479-1 (pbk); ISBN 978-1-118-49391-5 (ebk); ISBN 978-1-118-49392-2 (ebk); 978-1-118-49393-9 (ebk)

Manufactured in the United States of America

10 9 8 7 6 5 4 3 2 1

WILEY